Race, Gender, and Deviance in Xbox Live

Race, Gender, and Deviance in Xbox Live

Theoretical Perspectives from the Virtual Margins

Kishonna L. Gray

Series Editor
Victor E. Kappeler

AMSTERDAM • BOSTON • HEIDELBERG • LONDON
NEW YORK • OXFORD • PARIS • SAN DIEGO
SAN FRANCISCO • SINGAPORE • SYDNEY • TOKYO

Anderson Publishing is an imprint of Elsevier

Anderson Publishing is an imprint of Elsevier
225 Wyman Street, Waltham, MA 02451, USA
The Boulevard, Langford Lane, Kidlington, Oxford, OX5 1GB, UK

Notices
Knowledge and best practice in this field are constantly changing. As new research and experience broaden our understanding, changes in research methods, professional practices, or medical treatment may become necessary.

Practitioners and researchers must always rely on their own experience and knowledge in evaluating and using any information, methods, compounds, or experiments described herein. In using such information or methods they should be mindful of their own safety and the safety of others, including parties for whom they have a professional responsibility.

To the fullest extent of the law, neither the Publisher nor the authors, contributors, or editors, assume any liability for any injury and/or damage to persons or property as a matter of products liability, negligence or otherwise, or from any use or operation of any methods, products, instructions, or ideas contained in the material herein.

Library of Congress Cataloging-in-Publication Data
A catalog record for this book is available from the Library of Congress

British Library Cataloguing-in-Publication Data
A catalogue record for this book is available from the British Library

ISBN: 978-0-323-29649-6

For information on all Anderson publications visit
our website at store.elsevier.com

This book has been manufactured using Print On Demand technology. Each copy is produced to order and is limited to black ink. The online version of this book will show color figures where appropriate.

Working together
to grow libraries in
developing countries

ELSEVIER   Book Aid International

www.elsevier.com • www.bookaid.org

CONTENTS

PART III THE SOLUTIONS

ACKNOWLEDGMENTS

This book represents the culmination of a journey, the peak, the apex, my academic trek examining the experiences of women and people of color in Xbox Live. The basis of this book stemmed from my dissertation *Deviant Bodies Resisting Online: Examining the Intersecting Realities of Women of Color in Xbox Live*. This would not have been possible if it were not for the dedication of my dissertation committee—Lisa Anderson, Pauline Hope Cheong, and Merlyna Lim. Their valuable feedback was so instrumental to the success of this project. Lisa Anderson represents what every graduate student should have—a chair that recognizes when to step in to offer guidance and direction and when to allow room to interrogate new ideas. The balance she implemented allowed me to explore the breadth and depth of this topic as well as examine my own personal experiences inside this community. I must also thank Pauline and Merlyna for joining me on this journey and providing their expertise within the fields of technology, communication, and critical media studies. They encouraged me and instilled pride in this area when so many ignore these marginalized stories. They aided me in finding my calling in exploring race, gender, and new media. I would not have been able to complete this project without their invaluable expertise and guidance.

This project would not have been possible without the support of the series editor, Victor E. Kappeler. Thanks for taking a chance on this much needed manuscript. I must also thank the faculty, staff, and students in the College of Justice and Safety at Eastern Kentucky University for their continued feedback and support.

Also a special thanks to the School of Social Transformation and the Graduate School at Arizona State University for providing me with a Dissertation Completion grant. I'd still be sitting in my closet we called an office if it weren't for those funds. Thanks so much!

I must also thank the many scholars in the field who made this work possible with their trailblazing contributions and advice provided along the way: Anna Everette, David Leonard, Daniel Bernardi,

Andre Brock, Lisa Nakamura, Beth Kolko, Paul Barrett, Dean Chan, Radhika Gajjala, Tanner Higgin, T.L. Taylor, Tom Beollstorff, Danah Boyd, Mary L. Gray, and many, many others. Please let's continue this important work.

And to my graduate students for their last-minute edits and feedback, Bethany Nelson, Melissa Pujol, Emily Hayden, and Josh Hughes: you guys are the best.

I also have to thank my beautiful family—Kayland, Anteaus, and Anastacia. Y'all are my inspiration. When I feel like I can't think of another word to type, I look at your beautiful faces and am reminded of why I do what I do. Without you, this would be pointless. And to the Gray and Denson families and all of its extensions (Hall, Smith, Martin, Tate, just to name a few): I wouldn't be here if it weren't for the sacrifices you made along the way. When the lights were being turned off or when the rent couldn't get paid, you were right there helping us along the way. We may not be able to ever repay you, but just know, we are forever grateful for your love and support. And who knows, maybe the book will go platinum!

Started from the bottom...

AUTHOR BIOGRAPHY

Dr. Kishonna L. Gray is an assistant professor in the School of Justice Studies at Eastern Kentucky University in Richmond, KY. She completed her Ph.D. in justice studies at Arizona State University with a concentration in media, technology, and culture. Her research and teaching interests incorporate an intersecting focus on marginalized identities (race, gender, class, sexuality, citizenship, etc.) and new media (online news forums, social media, and virtual gaming communities). She has published in a variety of outlets including *Ada: A Journal of Gender, New Media, & Technology*, *New Review of Hypermedia and Multimedia*, *Crime, Media, Culture*, the *Bulletin of Science, Technology, & Society*, *Information, Communication, & Society*, and the *Journal of International and Intercultural Communication*.

Dismantling the Master's (Virtual) House:
One Avatar at a Time

If the twentieth century was the golden age of film, a time when Hollywood sought to unify (white) America through imagined narratives, nostalgia, and a constructed world based in American Exceptionalism, the twenty-first century will undoubtedly be the era of video games. Video games, as an interactive enterprise, represent the most sophistical, virtual form of fantastic play. They offer billions of game enthusiasts, located throughout the world, the opportunity to become a gangsta, a professional athlete, an explorer, a freedom fighter, a US Marine, a member of the Mafia, or even a white supremacist. They offer white middle-class youth the ability to experience the Other, to virtually transport themselves into an imagined world of play and pleasure. From the privacy of one's own home, game players are able to transport themselves into foreign and dangerous environments, often garnering pleasure through the domination and control of weaker characters of color. Video games, thus, operate as a sophisticated commodity that plays on peoples' desire to experience the Other, breaking down real boundaries between communities, between the real and the unreal, all while normalizing racial and gendered stereotypes, hegemonic narratives of the United States, and those practices that sanction virtual, sonic, and simulated violence faced by communities of color. Games matter not because they are fantasy that generates billions of dollars, or because they are a distraction or a utopia; they are not a joke or a world of make-believe, but pedagogical tools that in the end sanction and justify violence.

When I first started writing and researching on video games, there were not that many of us doing the work. Few and far between, the study of video games was not only peripheral to most academic discourses but also dismissed as boutique and "silly kid's stuff." For those of us working on race, gender, and video games, the visibility and respect was in short supply. The field of game studies and the interest in researching the pedagogies of video games was emergent albeit emerging in the face of institutional, industry, and fan-created obstacles. In fact, we surely could have put every scholar thinking about racial and gender representations within video games within a *Crazy Taxi*. In 2006, I wrote the following with the hopes that the next generation, those who are members of the Nintendo Generation or those who are members of Generation Wii, would not only take video games seriously and examine the pedagogies of race and gender, but more importantly advance these important discussions:

Beyond the fact that "the largely white male elite owners ... derive wealth from the circulation" of racist and sexist imagery, virtual reality and its inscription of controlling images "make racism, sexism and poverty appear to be natural, normal and inevitable part of everyday life" (Collins, 2000, p. 69). As argued by Mark Anthony Neal, "The fact that these images are then used to inform public policy around domestic images that adversely affect and black and brown people"—the war on terror, policing the border, welfare reform, the military industrial complex, global imperialism, the existence of the welfare state, the prison industrial complex, unemployment, etc.—"further complicates what is at stake" for game studies (Neal, 2005, p. 51). We do not need to continue game studies if such questions and realities are ignored. So, why game studies now? Because the refusal to engage critically such "kid stuff" has dire consequences, whether with domestic policy debates—more police, more prisons, less welfare—or foreign policy decisions—more bombs, more soldiers, less diplomacy. Video games teach, inform, and control, mandating our development of tools of virtual literacy, to expand pedagogies of games as part of a larger discursive turn to (and within) game studies. We need to teach about games since games are teaching so much about us ... and "them."

Dr. Kishonna Gray's *Race, Gender, and Deviance in Xbox Live: Theoretical Perspectives from the Virtual Margins* heeds this call, interrupting the regularly scheduled "it's just a game narrative." This work and her scholarship is a testament to how far we have come in terms of the conversations about games and gaming culture; yet her efforts to highlight persistent racism and sexism are also a sobering reminder of the work that needs to be done within game studies, particular as it relates to the experiences of women of color gamers. It is a call to action to address the normalization of sexist and racist violence within these online communities.

Our discussions of gaming culture always must begin with the assumption that video games are more than a playful diversion. Indeed, video games not only afford a unique and important space in which to think critically about representation, narrative, human beliefs, and behaviors, but they also direct attention to the centrality of race, gender, and nation; they offer a window into persistent stereotypes, political debates, and an insatiable desire for all things violent.

Spotlighting the representational stakes, and the impact of microaggressions, violence, and bigotry within online culture, Dr. Kishonna Gray offers an important bridge between those who have looked at stereotypes within gaming culture and those investing in looking at the experiences of gamers. Focusing on the racism and sexism experienced by Xbox gamers of color, and the intertwined nature of misogynistic and white supremacist narratives, images, and identities, Dr. Gray challenges readers to move beyond the binary. Those stereotypical images and representations, the hegemonic narratives of video games as a white space, alongside sonic profiling, racist comments, and other macro aggressions, contribute to a virtual world that is as unjust and troubling as its "real world counterparts."

As evidenced in this book, video games exist on a number of planes. At one level, games are commodities that generate billions of dollars; they are a cultural product bought and sold for profit, used to sell other products and lifestyles. Games are, thus, part of a world economy. At another level, games fulfill the insatiable desire of escape and fantasy. They offer their players the ability to enter a new world of excitement and pleasure.

Yet at another connected level, games are about race and gender. As with much of popular culture, they offer a "safe" space to discuss and consume stereotypical ideas about race and gender. They exist as a means to circulate accepted stereotypes of the OTHER, all while creating spaces to normalize those representations while disciplining those who seek to challenge the hegemonic organization of gaming culture. In this regard, games represent the circulation of once "private" but now public jokes and prejudices; they represent a vehicle for the dissemination of slurs; they represent the convergence of the front and back stages of racism and sexism (Picca & Feagin, 2007), the opportunity to perform and embody the powers and privileges afforded to whiteness and masculinity.

Finally, games are inherently political. As in other forms of genre fiction, video games are places where some of the political currents in society are explored in powerful ways, often beneath the radar of intellectuals and radical thinkers because they simply do not play or indulge in kids' leisure activities. This book fills all of these gaps, exploring all aspects of video game culture.

More than 10 years later after I started writing about video games, scholars and commentators continue to advance conversations in important ways. With *Race, Gender, and Deviance in Xbox Live* Dr. Kishonna Gray highlights the important advances in the discussion of video games, demonstrating the importance of this work. This book bridges cultural studies and game studies, ethnic studies and women's studies, academic and online debates, bringing these games into conversation with Patricia Hill Collins, Audre Lorde, Michael Omi and Howard Winant, Paul Gilroy, Stuart Hall, and countless others. It pushes the conversations beyond stereotypes toward an examination of power, intersectionality, the dialectics of discursive and textual, ideology, and the entrenched privilege of video game culture.

Games and gaming culture not only reflect entrenched inequality and lived male/white privilege but serve as an important instrument in the reproduction of hegemony. "By examining video game content through the eyes of the marginalized, by highlighting the virtual gaming experiences of minorities, and by interrogating possible solutions to intersecting oppressions," Dr. Gray provides "a much needed addition to theoretically examining video games, particularly Xbox Live, from a critical perspective." Building on a tradition of critical game studies, and voices that have long resisted the hegemonic representations available within gaming culture, *Race, Gender, and Deviance in Xbox Live* moves the conversation in important ways, focusing on the ways that black and brown bodies, those of women, are imagined as deviant, suspect, and undesirable in the games and in their spaces of play. Integrating a discussion of gaming communities, and the online turn in console games, this work pushes the conversation in important ways.

Race, Gender, and Deviance in Xbox Live, thus, takes readers on a journey from *Grand Theft Auto: San Andreas* to *Resident Evil 5*, from *Tomb Rader* to Xbox gamer communities, highlighting the "convergence" of multiple cultures and ideologies. Over the last 15 years, the technology and game playability may have changed; the aesthetics and popularity are dramatically different from a decade ago, yet as evidenced racial and gendered narratives have remained entrenched within virtual (and real) spaces. Claims of a postracial or a gender-neutral America, or celebrations of a "democratic" or transformative online culture notwithstanding, the video game industry and the players who inhabit these online communities continue to exhibit a "penchant for deploying ideologies from a hegemonic standpoint" (p. 16, Chapter 1). Evidence in a spectrum of video game representations and the normalized racial and gendered violence within these gaming communities, the importance of race and gender is not simply evident in the narratives, coding, or the flattened representations but in the avatars, in the policing that takes place between power, and the cashed-in privilege from dominant gamers. The continued significance of race and the persistent importance of gender isn't simply seen but felt, heard, and endured by gamers each and every day.

This work not only provides readers with important insights as to the persistent racism and sexism within video game culture, but arms readers with the tools of change. Spotlighting acts of resistance from gamers of color, and particularly women of color gamers, *Race, Gender, and Deviance in Xbox Live* provides a roadmap for combatting the violence, the stereotypes, the efforts to silence and erase gamers of color, and to otherwise work to create a more just virtual world. As Dr. Kishonna Gray reminds us, "Using the master's tools" provides a way to re-center racism, sexism, and other inequalities, but this does not mean that the tools can tear these 'isms' apart. ... " Yet challenging slurs and violence within gaming communities, yet disrupting racist and sexist representations that saturate the video game industry, yet demanding that the voices, and analysis of women of color, whether it be gamers or scholars, puts a crack in the virtual master's house. This book, and the conversations that it will produce, will continue the process of dismantling and challenging the hegemonic realities that sustain the master's house.

As I try to finish writing this foreword, the verdict in the trial of Michael Dunn has just been announced. Dunn shot and killed Jordan Davis, claiming that he "feared for his life." While Dunn was found guilty of several lesser-included charges, the jury was unable to reach a verdict in the murder charge. The verdict, 6 months after a Florida jury found George Zimmerman innocent in the killing of Trayvon

Martin, and in a year that saw the deaths of Renisha McBride and Jonathan A. Ferrell, reveals the entrenched realities, and life and death consequences of antiblack racism. The problem of the twenty-first century remains racism; from the ubiquitous practice of racial profiling to stand-your-ground laws to the ways that we narrate innocence and guilt; from the persistence of racist stereotypes to the differential value placed on and varied levels of sympathy afforded to black bodies, race matters. It matters in the criminal justice system and in the sphere of politics. It matters when looking at popular culture. It matters when examining video games, which continue to criminalize black bodies. The death of Jordan Davis and the refusal of a criminal justice system to find his killer guilty of murder is yet another reminder of the consequences of a society that sees no value in black life, that sees pleasure in black death, that sees blackness as interchangeable with "thug," and "criminal" (Russell, 1998), that sees black bodies as a source of "cultural degeneracy" and "a problematic sign and ontological position" (Williams, 1998, p. 140). The virtual and the everyday realities of America in the twenty-first century are all too connected. #ForJordan

David J. Leonard
February 15, 2014

WORKS CITED

Collins, P. H. (2000). *Black feminist thought: Knowledge, consciousness, and the politics of empowerment* (2nd ed.). New York, NY: Routledge.

Leonard, D. J. (2006). Not a hater, Just keepin' it real: The importance of race and gender based game studies. *Games and Culture*, *1*(1), 83–88.

Neal, M. A. (2005). *New black man*. New York, NY: Routledge.

Picca, L. H., & Feagin, J. R. (2007). *Two-faced racism: Whites in the backstage and frontstage*. New York, NY: Routledge.

Russell, K. K. (1998). *The color of crime: Racial hoaxes, white fear, black protectionism, police harassment, and other macroaggressions*. New York, NY: New York University Press.

Williams, R. (1998). Living at the crossroads: Exploration in race, nationality, sexuality, and gender. In W. Lubiano (Ed.), *The house that race built* (pp. 136–156). New York, NY: Vintage Books.

INTRODUCTION

My journey begins the same as it always has, in the comfort of night with the sounds of light whirring and warmth emitting gently in my direction. It's almost soothing, white noise to a baby's ear. I continue along and enter the world of Sera. I'm not alone. There are others who have embarked on this journey with me. We group ourselves together so we don't have to continue as individuals and become a collective, a team. We are just a group of people gathered for one cause, to save the world.

We organize ourselves for safety and many begin to talk strategy. The number one goal: stay alive! Several in the group begin talking and it's obvious one has emerged as our leader. I listen attentively and pay attention to the directions given. My first task, guard a particular area and prevent our foe from nabbing a certain weapon. My efforts were not successful. This led to the demise of my entire team, and I was disappointed I could not put up more of a fight to defeat the enemy. Fortunately for us, this magical world allows us to come back to life and giving us another chance to avenge our deaths.

We begin in another location and once again I am given instructions to help serve the team. This time, I am tasked with the safety of the leader. So I follow him and provide support. He runs naively into the opponent and I follow him as a good teammate would. It is a trick. We are flanked and killed, and I am blamed for this failure once again although our team emerges victorious.

The leader begins talking rather harshly to me and is upset that I am not engaging with the team or responding to his questions. So as to not aggravate him further, I insert my microphone and begin talking. I start off by apologizing for my failures and pledge to do better. However, this conversation shifts away from my poor performance within battle to attacks against me as a person.

"Oh you guys hear this? That's why you suck. You're a fucking girl! What the fuck are you doing in my room?" Even after this initial attack, I am still apologetic hoping that the attacks will soon end (at this point, I am used to the name calling). However, the attacks get worse.

"Wait wait wait. You're not just any girl. You're black. Get this black bitch off my team. Did you spend all your welfare check buying this game? Why aren't you doing what you love? Get back to your crack pipe with your crack babies." The insults continue with a barrage of colorful stereotypical comments aimed at me as an African-American woman. The beautiful world I begin discussing is not so beautiful all the time. The journey, although mostly fun and enjoyable, frequently becomes a place full of hatred and intolerance. This journey I am referring to is the online gaming experience associated with Xbox Live.

(Gray, 2011, pp. 1—2)

The above excerpt highlights my personal experiences gaming in Xbox Live as a woman of color within a space so often constructed as a space for white males. Within these next few pages, I will highlight an often overlooked aspect of gaming and that's examining the margins where women and people of color game on a regularly basis. By examining video game content through the eyes of the marginalized, by highlighting the virtual gaming experiences of minorities, and by interrogating possible solutions to intersecting oppressions, this book will be a much needed addition to the theoretical examination of video games, particularly Xbox Live, from a critical perspective.

I.1 XBOX AS A MEDIATED CONSOLE MULTIPLAYER ENVIRONMENT

Xbox has proven to be more than just a gaming platform for users. It has evolved into a multimedia entertaining outlet for more than 20 million users. The nature of the space distinguishes it from other video games (e.g., Everquest, World of Warcraft) and gaming environments (e.g., Massively Multiplayer Online, Massively Multiplayer Online Role-Playing Game, etc.). There are several features that distinguish Xbox/Xbox Live from its other gaming counterparts: (1) the game is mediated through a console not a computer; (2) online connectivity is not a requirement to game although it is required to access online features; (3) when connected to the Internet (on Xbox Live), there is the option to explore other mediated content other than just gaming; and (4) Xbox Live users aren't necessarily gamers; some purchase the console to satisfy other entertainment needs. Before unpacking the characteristics associated with Xbox/Xbox Live, it is important to properly situate Xbox/Xbox Live within the world of gaming and entertainment.

> As Henry Jenkins (2006) explains, we live in an era of convergence: technological, economic, aesthetic, organic, global—and they all intersect to redefine and reconstruct how we interact with mediated environments. One such mediated environment is Xbox Live which has evolved from a mere console video game to a massive entertainment outlet providing games, movies, TV, music, social networking, and more.
>
> (Gray, 2012, p. 463)

The above quotation reflects the need to redefine how we interrogate console gaming environments such as Xbox Live. A term that encompasses the nature of seventh-generation console video games is

Mediated Console Multiplayer Environment (MCME). By incorporating old and new media to provide choice for the gaming audience, Microsoft Xbox Live, Sony Playstation Network, and Nintendo Network (formerly Nintendo Wi-Fi Connection) have situated themselves to reach millions of individuals who may not necessarily be gamers, but who may decide to utilize the console to satisfy varying entertainment and functional needs (Gray, 2012). As Quinn (2005) highlights, the popularity of media convergence originates from the need to reach as many individuals as possible to grant them unlimited access to information whenever and wherever they want it. Although Quinn was referring to news media, the statement readily applies to other entities striving for convergence. MCMEs have continuously repositioned themselves as a convergent medium and have successfully maintained a following of users (particularly true for Xbox and Playstation). In January 2009, Xbox Live boasted 17 million members (Thorsen, 2009), and in February 2010, Xbox Live had reached 23 million registered users (Whitten, 2010). Although the purpose of this text is to examine interactions within a virtual community, some background is needed to situate the audience within this gaming space.

I.1.1 Features of Xbox/Xbox Live

In order to become a member of Xbox Live, a membership must be purchased. After the membership is purchased, the player decides on a gamertag. The gamertag is a player's username within Xbox Live. The tag can be up to 15 characters in length. Images are also associated with gamers and their gamertags. These images can be user-uploaded, purchased and downloaded, or can be an image of the avatar created within the space. The avatar within the Xbox Live context is a visual representation that the gamer creates. As Gray (2011) explains, avatars can sometimes embody the player's offline presence in this gaming space, although some people opt for an avatar bearing no resemblance to the self. Literature on the avatar is largely dependent on the type of game that is being played, but Yee (2004) explains that the avatar is simply a projection or idealization of the gamer's own identity, an experimentation of a new identity, or a pawn. In many computer games, avatars are animal representations, and in other games, the avatar is pre-created and the user simply selects the graphic representation of his or her choice (Webb, 2001). Many virtual communities such as Xbox Live have pre-created avatars, although they are heavily stereotyped along the lines of race and ethnicity. As Webb (2001) explains, the avatar usually appears as ethnically white with mundane aspects of masculinity and femininity being vividly marked out. Although outside of the scope of this text, scholars are beginning to devote significant attention to nonverbal forms of communication within virtual communities as the avatar and gamertag are included in this category (Gray & Buente, 2014). The role of the avatar also depends on type of game. For instance, in computer games, the avatar is usually the playable character within the game. In Webb's (2001) study on the cybercommunity *Virtual Places*, avatars have the ability to:

> ...tour the virtual environment, visit chat rooms, electronic shopping malls, personalized websites and game environments. They talk and gesture to each other in either open public or private rooms. At any one time there are approximately 650 rooms being occupied by participants in Virtual Places. The personalized avatars are under the control of an individual user. Control is through the mouse, which enables the user to point at things and issue commands. Talking is accomplished by typing at the keyboard. (p. 564)

I.2 COMMUNICATION AND CONFLICT IN XBOX LIVE

Microsoft Xbox has implemented several upgrades to the system to reduce the verbal abuse experienced in the game (as will be discussed in the following chapters). One upgrade in particular, gamer zones, was introduced, which would only allow players to interact with other gamers who match their playing style (Xbox Live, 2009). The types of gamer zones included: Recreation, Family, Pro, and Underground. Gamers select these zones based on the description given when creating the profile. "Recreation" is for casual gamers. "Family" is for gamers who prefer a family safe zone. "Pro" is for competitive gamers who enjoy a challenge, and "Underground" is for gaming where anything goes as long as it does not violate the Xbox Live Terms of Use (Xbox Live, 2009). In practice, these gamer zones did not live up to their purpose as they didn't affect gameplay or the matching of players in online games (Xbox Live, 2009).

Xbox also utilizes a feedback system that allows gamers to file complaints about others through the system. This is another upgrade for which the results haven't matched the intended purpose. There were further upgrades to Xbox Live implemented in November 2008. This upgrade was called the "New Xbox Experience" and featured the addition of Netflix and other types of applications, the forced creation of avatars, and the introduction of the party chat system allowing gamers to enter a private chat room (Geddes, 2008). The party system has actually proven useful for gamers who experience discrimination in the Xbox space, allowing them to self-segregate from the larger gaming community. Gamers can stay away from players they choose to avoid. However, this creates a problem in addressing meaningful solutions to verbal abuse within this space. Segregating gamers does nothing to offset the verbal abuse inherent in the space.

Although communication within the space is the origin of many problems in Xbox Live, it is also a defining feature that sets Xbox apart from other gaming spaces. As was previously mentioned, there are messaging options as well as multiple levels of private and public chat. Many users of this gaming space express that the use of a headset and voice capabilities is a "step forward in game development" (Wadley, Gibbs, Hew, & Graham, 2003, p. 40). Comparing computer gaming, many prefer the hands-free feature as opposed to the text-based model in many computer video games. Most players utilize the voice chat, but as was witnessed in the participation observations, the presence of voice is the origin of conflict within this space. The nature of social interactions within Xbox Live, which are often riddled with deviant behavior including but not limited to racism and sexism, must be studied.

I.3 THE MARGINALIZED AS GAMER

It has been stated that we have entered a postracial, postfeminist society, suggesting that we have moved beyond notions of race-, gender-, and sexuality-based discrimination (Joseph, 2009, p. 238). Cyberspace is deemed an even more utopic space being dubbed the "new frontier" waiting to be settled by opportunistic travelers of the virtual world. Brookey (2009) warns us about viewing this space as the new American frontier, recalling the oppression and domination that emerged from opening up the original, physical frontier (Gray, 2011). Racial minorities served as the labor force needed to open up that frontier but rarely were able to enjoy the benefits of their labor. This view translates into the console gaming space as well when you take a look at who the gaming industry targets. McQuivey (2001) suggests that as games are developed, they continually aim to fulfill the perceived desires of the young, middle-class male who is supposedly the market's target. Disturbingly absent from discussions on video game markets is the fact that young black and Latino youths assisted in propelling the video gaming industry into the million-dollar industry by spending time and money in arcades (Everett, 2009). This could be due to the power structure of the gaming industry being a predominately white, and secondarily Asian, male-dominated elite (Fron, Fullerton, Morie, & Pearce, 2007). The hegemonic elite has excluded and alienated minority players who in numerical terms actually constitute a majority (Fron et al., 2007). This majority consists of female gamers, people of different racial and cultural backgrounds, and gamers of varying ages. This also includes gamers who utilize multiple platforms in which to game—mobile phones, hand-held devices, console games, computer games, gaming applications, and so on. Everett (2009) also confirms from her work on video game cover art that those invested in the gaming industry, including popular media, not only depict the typical gamer as male but also as white (p. 111).

I.3.1 "Girl Gamers"

Video gaming has traditionally been framed as an activity for males. But the number of females who play video games or consider themselves gamers has increased consistently over the last decade. According to the Entertainment Software Association's (ESA) 2012 video and computer game industry report, of all video game players, approximately 47% are female, which is increased over the 2008 industry report of only 40% of all gamers being female. Furthermore, of all the female gamers, women aged 18 or older represent a significantly greater portion of the game-playing population (30%) than boys aged 17 or younger (18%) (Entertainment Software Association, 2008, 2012). Although the number of female gamers is increasing, there are still genres of gaming that are dominated by male gamers. Examples of genres still dominated by males include: First-Person Shooters (FPS), Role-Playing Games (RPG), and other types of Massively Multiplayer Online Games (MMOG). Although these genres are still dominated by males, women are slowly entering these spaces and are creating their own communities to game with other women. Some refer to these gaming communities as clans.

As Peña (2013) explains, clans can be considered as teams within the communities. Early clans began with the Personal Computer Local Area Networks (PC LAN) in the 1990s, with games such as *Quake* and *Doom*, among others. These LAN parties, as they came to be known, were a place where clan members could meet and practice to game at public events such as DreamHack in Jönköping, Sweden (currently the largest

LAN party in the world) and BYOC (Bring Your Own Computer), a very large LAN party held in New Delhi, India (Peña, 2013). However, the number of gaming clans significantly increased and their purpose drastically changed in the early 2000s with the incorporation of the Internet onto gaming consoles.

> At these types of parties, it would be common to see eight consoles (e.g., Xbox/Xbox 360) linked together through an LAN playing games like Halo. When Halo 2 was introduced in 2004, Xbox allowed the creation of gaming clans, up to 100 members, to play the first-person shooter style MMO competitively. It was during this time that I was first introduced to the existence of an all-female gaming clan.
>
> (Peña, 2013, p. 2)

All-female gaming clans operate similar to their male counterparts, but their purpose and motivation sometimes drastically vary, as this text will highlight. Because women are perceived to be invading the men's locker room, there is much conflict that women sometimes want to avoid.

Gamers are not alone in creating this gender conflict. The video game industry has been directly complicit in creating an atmosphere that excludes and ostracizes female gamers. This is also not just situated within the Microsoft context. As Lee McEnany Caraher, Sega spokesperson, stated, they just haven't yet decided to focus marketing efforts on female gamers. As he stated, "Maybe we should spend time marketing to girls. We just haven't chosen to, because the bigger part of the market is boys. The girls are secondary. They come after" (Peña, 2013, p. 2). He furthered by stating that marketing is not geared towards girls because of the differential consumption patterns between males and females (girls think too much about their purchases). There was even a difference in discussing gender differences among hard-core gamers, suggesting it was still an all-male domain with sprinkles of women throughout. This is evident in how games are created and advertised. There are just not enough women involved in the creation of video games, and as Hafner (2004) illustrates, only 10% of all game industry workers are women and most of them do not even have any influence on the design process. The problem arises when a masculine entity attempts to incorporate women; they don't know how.

As Flanagan (2005) examines, there are a few reasons explaining why so few women choose science- and technology-related fields.

Reasons include: (1) a lack of female role models; (2) girls' underdeveloped spatial visualization skills; and (3) learning styles that are incompatible with the methods practiced by men (as cited in Wyatt, 1993). These reasons are valid, but one key component that is missing is the sexism and structure of masculinity that is embedded in certain fields and industries that lead to a hostile environment for many women and people of color.

I.3.2 Gamers of Color

There is a common misconception of minority gamers that they are not in fact true gamers. Interestingly, a 2011 Nielsen survey found that black gamers actually spent the most time of any demographic playing console video games (Good, 2011). This mythical assumption is also evident in the limited amount of academic scholarship devoted to the topic. So to highlight the issues that minority gamers face, this text will add to the literature an examination of their experiences and their responses to oppressions.

Much of the information that is available on the experiences of minority gamers stems from the online communities that minority gamers have created. A defining discussion that influenced the direction of this work stemmed from a blog posted by A.B. Frasier, cofounder of the Koalition, a video game website catering to urban and hip–hop communities. Frasier elaborates on the myth specifically relating to blacks playing within gaming communities:

> ...when you have the video game media not show so much color then of course something like "black people don't play video games" gets spat out from a idiots mouth. The major media doesn't have any personalities that shows gaming from an urban perspective, therefore we don't exist in many people's eyes...You can call me a nigger, porch monkey or whatever, but I'm still a gamer.
>
> (Frasier, 2009)

Frasier highlights two important issues that this textbook will discuss: (1) the video gaming industry has all but ignored minority gamers in character, video game content, and advertising; and (2) the default gamer has yet to welcome minority gamers, often lashing out in inflammatory ways within the virtual gaming space. As has been highlighted, the origins of conflict within Xbox Live, and most virtual communities that employ verbal communications, linguistic profiling. These concepts will be interrogated and explored throughout this text.

PART I

The Games

CHAPTER 1

Video Games as Ideological Projects

CJ left the 'hood to start a new life, or rather, a new life of crime. But the death of his mother in a drive-by shooting beckoned him to return to the Grove. While away in Liberty City, CJ began working in the car theft business, honing his skills, which would soon come in handy. Upon his return to Los Santos after five years of being gone, CJ is confronted by members of the highly corrupt C.R.A.S.H., Community Resources Against Street Hoodlums, an anti-gang unit of the Los Santos Police Department. They coerce CJ into informing for them, with the threat of his being framed for killing one of their fellow police officers. CJ complies after realizing that his former neighborhood gang, the Grove Street Family, has lost much of its power and notoriety since he left and this would be a good way to keep the police at bay. CJ works to start rebuilding the gang while slaughtering dozens in the process. He eventually achieves his goal of rebuilding the Grove Street Family, and becomes a wealthy business owner in the process.

This brief overview of Carl Johnson, the protagonist of Grand Theft Auto: San Andreas, reveals a life full of crime, violence, and death. This narrative has become a common media trope to describe black America. What this story, among hundreds of others, represents is a normalized violence in the lives of many minorities in the United States. Rockstar, the producer of the popular Grand Theft Auto franchise, is known for satirizing much about American popular culture. This parody reveals much about how race, gender, and class are understood within popular culture.

There are three main reasons why I begin this chapter with the story of CJ from San Andreas. First, crime in CJ's life is ever-present. The audience is to assume that this is a normal way of life for him and his counterparts, without ever contextualizing structural discrimination leading to this reality. Second, the normalization reconfirms for mainstream America that crime and black America are synonymous, a common trend in media. Third, although this game proved that the default gamer could in fact be comfortable with playing a minority character, that character would have to exist within common frames that continue to stereotype the lives of black Americans. These three tenets will be unpacked in later chapters, but it is useful in setting the tone for the book.

1.1 RACE AND GENDER AS IDEOLOGY

Race and gender, as hierarchical structures, have manifested in video games in stereotypical manners that fit within the hegemonic notions of what it means to be a person of color or what it means to be a woman. Specifically, by employing Omi and Winant's (1994) conception of racial project, we can see how many popular video games fit within this theoretical schema wherein racialized ideas, bodies, and structures are constructed, mediated, and presented through a safe medium. Using their definition, race should not be understood in terms of physical or biological reality. Rather, race is created under conditions of power whereby historically one group dominates others politically, economically, and socially.

Omi and Winant describe a racial project simultaneously with interpretation, representation, or explanation of racial dynamics, and an effort to reorganize and redistribute resources along particular racial lines. Using the example from above to illustrate, *San Andreas* can be examined through the scope of a racial project operating as a hegemonic system. For Omi and Winant, hegemony is a popular system of ideas and practices enacted through all social institutions, including education, religions, and media.

> Race becomes common sense—a way of comprehending, explaining and acting in the world. A vast web of racial projects mediates between the discursive or representational means in which race is identified and signified on the one hand, and the institutional and organizational forms in which it is routinized and standardized on the other.
>
> **(Omi and Winant, 1994, p. 60)**

Race and racist practices are embedded into the social fabric of the American social order, validating racialized practices in many institutional settings, and video games are not exempt from this trend. The dominant narratives deployed in video games such as Halo, Call of Duty, Street Fighter, Gears of War, Grand Theft Auto, and others lead to the continued construction and maintenance of hegemonic masculinity and whiteness as privilege. By using narrative research as a means to study the content of these video games, I am able to establish the link between narrative and hegemonic ideology.

1.2 VIDEO GAME NARRATIVE

Narrative has recently gained the attention of social scientists as an analytical framework. Its strength lies not as a singular method of analysis, but rather an area of inquiry that is inclusive of a variety of approaches to privilege the experiences of the marginalized. Broadly, narrative research can be understood as any study that uses or analyzes narrative materials by creating a model that can be used for the analysis of a wide spectrum of narratives. Narrative, in the current context, will be applied throughout this text to analyze popular video games and the cultural representations deployed therein. My focus is not on the larger debate surrounding gameplay versus narrative, but rather on what is actually being deployed through the story line and imagery of these video games creating the narrative.

As Juul (2002) argues, games can be compared to traditional narrative media, and compares the experience of playing a computer game to an actor's performance in a film or play. This imitation of film and cinema has increased in video games with advancing technologies which allow these capabilities. But more importantly, many modern video games operate from a first or third person viewpoint and require the audience member (gamer) to control the progression of the story (although there is no control over the preconstructed narrative). This direct immersion into gameplay makes focusing on what the audience is consuming even more compelling. There is a strong emotional resonance that gamers have with the interactivity of gameplay. This emotional connection to gameplay illustrates that as the story line for a game gets stronger, the less players can influence it, actually increasing their emotional attachment. Understanding the structure of narrative will move toward an understanding of the power they have to deploy particular ideologies.

Importantly, there are three structural features of narratives: event structure, evaluative system, and explanatory system. An important tool in narrative analysis is the examination of events that are selected for narration as well as those which are omitted. The evaluative structure creates the reality and normalizes the way things are and the way things ought to be. So narrative is linked closely to ideology, specifically about what is included and what is omitted.

It is also important to recognize that all narratives contain within them an ideological project. This is an important feature of narratives, especially since they have the ability to bridge the gap between daily social interaction and large-scale social structures. However, what often occurs is that the narrative hides and makes invisible the operation of power relations masking the relationship between subjection and coercion. This politics of narrative allows us to examine the link between narrative and ideology in video games.

Scholars have identified the hegemonic potential of narrative by illustrating how narratives can contribute to the reproduction of existing structures of meaning and power. There are three important functions of narrative: (1) a means of social control, (2) a hegemonic process enhanced by the narratives' ability to colonize consciousness, and (3) a contributor to hegemony to the extent that they conceal the social organization of their production and plausibility. Because narratives depict specific individuals, cultures, locations, etc., they make sense of the world and become more powerful as they are constantly deployed and repeated. Ian Bogost (2006) suggests that this reinforcement is an important tool in perpetuating certain ideological projects in his examination of political discourse in video games. The rhetoric deployed relies heavily on our previous encounters with certain metaphoric language.

It is important to recognize that language cannot be separated from structures of ideology and power. As a society, we are conditioned from birth to consider things that are culturally acceptable, immediately encountering ideology. So language and the accepted signs within our culture become important means to accept certain things as normal at the expense of others. Society genders toys. We racially segregate ourselves. We engage in activities that situate us within certain classes and status. We can apply this same concept to video games. The ways that race and gender are deployed within video games highlights hegemonic notions of what it means to be black, Asian, female, etc. This ideology relayed through a medium consumed by millions of individuals proves to be dangerous especially when that imagery is stereotypical. It becomes true because it's constantly reinforced.

1.2.1 Ideology and Hegemony

Ideology refers to the collective of ideas that reflect the interests of a group of people. What has occurred in the United States context is that race and sex have infiltrated in such a way that these ideologies have been mainstreamed and have found themselves embedded in digital media and video gaming. The purpose of these images is to make intersecting inequalities appear to be natural, normal, and inevitable parts of everyday life. These normalized images continue to justify the oppression of marginalized and minority populations. One would think that debunking and challenging these images would be an easy feat. But these images have been generalized to the point of normalcy by the dominant group who holds the authority to define values within society and continue to proliferate, where images to counter these cannot compete.

Hegemony is a useful tool in understanding the process involved in maintaining this type of power. Hegemony according to Gramsci (1971) refers to an ideology, most often understood as "common sense" or "natural" that constitutes a form of cleverly masked, taken-for-granted domination. Hegemony can be understood as the process by which those who support the dominant ideology in a culture are able to continually reproduce that ideology in cultural institutions. Hegemony is not granted through coercive force but rather by consent from subordinate groups. Furthermore, domination relies on coercion while hegemony relies on the dominant group positioning itself as the leader with society's overall interest in mind. Hegemony thus involves the successful mobilization and reproduction of the active consent of dominated groups and constitutes an invisible prison of intersecting gazes to those who have little power to negotiate or even voice alternate stories defining and shaping their existence. Within the video gaming industry, the creators and producers of content are primarily white and male. They construct realities from their perspective of the world. Their realities are mediated and this mediation is far too often stereotypical and not truly representative of women or people of color.

Gramsci's concept of hegemony can be understood in the world of gaming. For Gramsci, ideology informs and shapes everyday life by leading toward an unquestioned common sense. This common sense is imposed on us without our conscious recognition. By using Gramsci (1971), we see how ruling groups aim to maintain a popular system of ideas and practices in which he called "common sense" which is used to gain consent for rule. Video games, in disseminating stereotypes, in offering bodies and spaces of color as sites of play, and in affirming dominant ideas about poverty, unemployment, crime, and war, contribute to the consolidation of white supremacist power. Ultimately, the images and ideologies offered through games elicit individual consent for structural policies, thereby legitimizing structures of whiteness and masculinity.

1.2.2 Examining Hegemonic Whiteness
Whiteness as an area of study was largely ignored until recent decades. Whiteness is a particular material, cultural, and subjective location in

the United States that "signals the production and reproduction of dominance rather than subordination, normativity rather than marginality, and privilege rather than disadvantage" (Frankenberg, 1993, pp. 236–237). Studies into whiteness examines that, for the most part, the experience of being white has gone unmarked and assumed. This invisibility of whiteness and lack of racial consciousness among whites are a key part of the privilege of being white, allowing them to treat whiteness as an apolitical characteristic rather than a significant social status. This is most often seen when whites attempt to describe their white identity. What occurs most often is that it is defined by what it is not. This is another example of white privilege, not only because whites do not have to define who they are or understand their racial identity but also because they do not have to have a full understanding of their status in relation to racial others to navigate society. Whiteness may be politicized both in terms of acknowledging racial privilege and prejudice and in denying these exist, at least individually. This is another way whites distinguish themselves by what they are not, by separating themselves from a racist conception of whiteness.

Because there are variations of whiteness, all marked by privilege and marginalization, and no identity is homogenous, it is important to note that the topic of discussion in this text is hegemonic whiteness. What I discuss throughout this text is referred to as the ideal type of whiteness that is dominant and thus considered normative and standard, all the while going unmarked. Scholars describe whiteness as an oppressive invention that has been, at different times and places, adopted, naturalized, reworked, and abandoned. Some argue, and I contend, that whiteness also reflects the extent and nature of class struggle. In the US context, it is middle and upper class whites who hold this hegemonic position because their material conditions and cultural practices most closely resemble the characteristics of hegemonic whiteness. Staying true to hegemony, even among this group, many among them may not completely match the ideal type of hegemonic whiteness, but their claim to authority aligns them with this position and gives them more power to define and sustain whiteness. In this analysis of whiteness, there is no denying that there are privileges associated with being white, but rather, I recognize that there are degrees of privilege that not all whites are able to take advantage of at any given time. This varying degree of whiteness is made obvious in Grand Theft Auto V through the playable characters of Michael De Santa and Trevor Phillips. (There is also a third playable character, an African-American male named Franklin Clinton.)

> I pay you to listen to my problems. I'm rich. I'm miserable. Half the time, my kids can't stand me. The other half, my wife is cheating on me. I kill people without remorse, Doc. Hell, I'm pretty average for this town, really (in game quote from Grand Theft Auto: V).

This in-game quote by playable character Michael De Santa reflects a parody of the elite and the rich in the United States. Michael, one of the three main protagonists, grew up poor and with abusive parents. This tough upbringing propelled him into a life of crime where he amassed his fortunes. After several stints in prison, Michael met Trevor Phillips and they began a criminal partnership with Michael the organizer and Trevor the executor.

Although Michael earned his fortunes engaging in criminal activity, the game does not showcase much of his previous life. What GTA:V shows is a rich white man living in a mansion dictating orders down to his marginalized partners. After faking his death and giving up Trevor in a heist gone bad, Michael received a comfortable stipend and was relocated to a large mansion in Los Santos (fictional Los Angeles) living with his wife, a former prostitute and stripper.

When we begin with Michael's portion of the story, his wife has spent much of his money, his children have no respect for him, and he is currently in the midst of a midlife crisis with frequent visits to a therapist. However, these hard facts of life do little to diminish his existence within the game. Although we play all three characters in an equal manner, they are by no means equal. Michael is obviously their leader and determines the criminal exploits of the group.

1.2.3 "Othering" Whiteness

On the other side of whiteness, Trevor Phillips visually is less affluent than his white counterpart Michael. What we know about his background comes directly from him within the game.

> [Trevor]..."grew up in five states, two countries, fourteen different homes, eight fathers, three care homes, two correctional facilities, one beautiful, damaged flower of a mother" and has "served time, my country, your country and myself."

His character is mostly marked by his rage, anger issues, and violent impulses that make it hard for him to have normal interactions. After the ill-fated heist where Michael faked his death, Trevor made a new life for himself in the rural town of Sandy Shores, San Andreas. He organizes a small criminal enterprise specializing in gun smuggling and manufacturing and distributing crystal meth. Although Trevor is not nearly as wealthy as Michael, he is by no means poor. However, staying true to parody, Rockstar successfully stereotypes Trevor's character as "poor white trash." His clothing is always dirty. The places he lives are always unkempt. His overall appearance, way of talking, and overall character are reflective of what society stereotypes of poor whites. Trevor, as a marginalized white, is admonished within the game for not representing whiteness as synonymous with material success and is thus seen as a lesser category of white. These two characters reflect the aforementioned degrees of whiteness. Although white is a privileged identity, not all whites are afforded the full knapsack of privilege associated with this constructed identity.

Dominant and elite whites have decided, hegemonically—not through force—what is important or significant. The process of "othering" within the white identity occurs by accepting a dualistic notion of culture: Whiteness comes to be an unmarked or neutral category whereas other cultures, such as poor white ones, are specifically marked (as redneck, poor white trash, etc.). Just as othering occurs in physical spaces, it also occurs in online communities.

Othering is here defined as the process of categorizing a person or group of people as belonging to an out group rather than an in group. This stems from our desire to belong to groups with which we identify (Tajfel & Turner, 1986). In the process of defining the group that one belongs to, it becomes necessary to determine what and who does not define or belong to the in group, thus delineating the "same" and the "other." The process of othering is what leads to the marginalization of certain groups and individuals. The medium of communication within video games is important in analyzing othering. Within video games, visually describing the other as different leads to marginalization, and in voice-based chat communities, auditory communication (linguistic profiling) leads to othering.

Cultural and rhetorical boundary work also serves to distinguish marginalized whites from one another based on real cultural practices and imposed cultural images. This marking functions to keep hegemonic whiteness pure because keeping it pure maintains and sustains an ideal type to be distinguished from others. So as we form our conceptualization of identity, sometimes it leads to misrepresentations and stereotyping of the "other." Identification, according to Hall (1996, p. 2), involves "recognition of some common origin or shared characteristics with another person or group." Identities always need to be placed in the historical context: they are not about "who we are" or "where we came from," but rather what we "might become, how we have been represented and how that bears on how we might represent ourselves" (Ibid). Hall points out that identity is constructed within, not outside of, representation and through, not outside of, difference and the relation to the "Other." Identities function as "points of identification and attachment only because of their capacity to exclude, to leave out, to render 'outside', abjected" (1996, p. 5). The process is fictional and imaginary, but nonetheless politically effective.

Constructions of white identity, as different from other racial identities, are primarily based on boundary work operating employing phrases such as "we're not that" or "we're not them." Scholars also recognize that whites employ boundary work to distinguish themselves from one another. The type of whiteness that is privileged at any one time and place often reflects the extent and nature of class struggle. To determine the limits or boundaries of whiteness, it is imperative to question the assumption that race and class always intersect to produce one type of white identity. In doing so, we are able to challenge the meaning of whiteness that is based on the notion implicit in scholarly and public discourse that race and class interact to "produce monolithic racial categories of privileged whites and disadvantaged minorities rather than diversely identified groups" (Gibson, 1996, p. 380).

The lived experiences of rural, Southern whites, whom Trevor's character is loosely based upon, visibly illustrate how race and class interact to produce varying constructions of whiteness. The terms "redneck" and "white trash" are stereotypical terms applied to subordinate whites and clearly illustrate intraracial boundary work. For example, these terms are often marked as "cultural" like other marginalized groups. Unfortunately, these marginalized whites are both excluded from and assimilated into hegemonic whiteness. Stereotyping is a form of representational practice that essentializes, reduces, and naturalizes people to a few simple traits and excludes everything that does not belong (Hall, 1997, p. 257). Hall points out that stereotyping sets up a symbolic frontier between the "normal" and the "deviant," the "normal" and the "pathological," the "acceptable" and the "unacceptable." It facilitates the "binding" or bonding together of all of Us who are "normal" into one "imagined community"; and it sends into symbolic exile all of Them—the "Others"—who are in some way different (p. 258). Hall (1996) explains that the key features of the discourse of the "Other" involve collapsing several characteristics into one simplified figure that represents the essence of the people, and then splitting the stereotype into its "good" and "bad" sides.

To construct their whiteness, hegemonic whites mark marginalized whites, who in turn, construct their whiteness by aligning with hegemonic whites in marking other racial groups, particularly blacks. To better articulate, marginalized whites mark blacks and other racial groups as "other" and "inferior" in order to feel superior and to cling to their "wages of whiteness" as their only access to power (Roediger, 1991). As a result,

> ...the redneck has never identified his real enemy, the Southern upper class (an ownership class enmeshed with 'outside' capitalists) and its sup-porting 'middle class,' though he is acutely aware of his insecurity in a land of plenty. ... The redneck has been reluctant, unfortunately, to admit his structural underclass status and therefore, has failed to identify with his own kind along social class lines.
>
> (Roebuck & Neff, 1980, p. 258)

This process keeps hegemonic whites in their dominant position, by using racism to pit similar class groups against each other. We form our identities in part by the process of defining and marginalizing the other. So if identities form in relation to "Others," representation gives them meaning. According to Hall, when we give others meaning through representation, we also get a sense of our own identity and of who we are.

> It is by our use of things, and what we say, think and feel about them—how we represent them—that we give them a meaning ... we give things meaning by how we represent them—the words we use about them, the stories we tell about them, the images of them we produce, the emotions we associate with them, the ways we classify and conceptualize them, the values we place on them.
>
> (Hall, 1997, p. 3)

This interconnected system of race and class is mostly invisible to those within it, especially marginalized whites. Because of their marked identity, marginalized whites may have much more sense of community and consciousness about being white than many other whites.

Figure 1.1 visualizes the process involved in "othering" marked identities. Hegemonic whiteness exists on top of the racial hierarchy with marked whiteness existing on the periphery of this elite status. Racial minorities constitute the bottom of the racial hierarchy having their identities constructing in opposition to whiteness.

1.2.4 Hegemonic Masculinity

Masculinity portrayed in video games must be understood through several lenses. By focusing our discussion on hegemonic masculinity, marginalized masculinities, and female objectification, I am able to create the context for examining the narrative and visual imagery deployed in contemporary video games.

Hegemonic masculinity blends Gramsci's analysis of class and power relations with feminist research about the ways gender relationships shape society (Connell, 2001; Levy, 2007). It is a theoretical perspective that explains how some men make it appear normal, natural, and necessary that they remain in a position of power over men and most women because they have always been in that position of power (Levy, 2007). Hegemonic masculinity takes as its basic foundation that women exist as potential sexual objects for men—they provide men with sexual validation—and that men compete with each other to attain those sexual objects. This basic premise was apparent with the release of the trailer advertising the 2013 release of Tomb Raider.

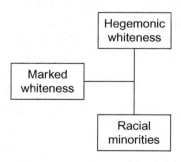

Figure 1.1 Racial hierarchy.

The trailer opens up dark and ominous, eventually panning to a young, bleeding Lara Croft. She is hanging upside down, bloody, dirty, and obviously injured. She eventually releases herself and explores the cave in which she is trapped. Danger quickly catches up to her, but she eludes further harm and is able to escape. The trailer highlights her physical ability, skill, and intellect problem solving to save herself and keep herself protected from harm as well as showing dedication to her friends. What the trailer also shows is a vulnerable woman who has to find a way to avoid sexual victimization. The trailer implies that Lara falls victim to sexual assault (although in the actual game she is not sexually victimized). The marketing team made a conscious decision to illustrate Lara in this manner based on real concerns selling the game with a female protagonist. A common argument is often made that the default gamer (white male) won't play characters that differ from his own identity because of his inability to relate to that character. This argument is often used to justify the lack of diversity among playable characters and that the gaming industry is out to reap profits. To sell Tomb Raider to males who would never play a female hero, the character had to become sexually vulnerable in order for males to identify with her—they become her protector. By deploying this common narrative of women within media as weak and in need of saving, the gaming industry maintains hegemonic masculinity. This constant narrative deployed generates the value of certain events, people, relationships, and actions. Importantly, these narrative schemas should not be viewed as records of fact or how things are/were; the creators of these narrative works have made sense of their experiences and perceptions and created digital realities based on these perceptions (Van Maanen, 1988).

1.2.5 Marginalized Masculinities

As Connell (2001) explains, at any given time, one form of masculinity may be culturally exalted over other forms of hegemonic masculinity. He also explains that the most powerful people in society may not be the most visible bearers of hegemonic masculinity, but rather that it is the successful claim to authority that is the mark of hegemony. Some men are able to align themselves with the public image of hegemonic masculinity, no matter how much their personal lives actually match this hegemonic pattern. Thus, hegemonic masculinity operates as an ideal type of masculinity that most, if not all, men cannot completely embody. However, some men are seen as further away from this ideal, and thus their masculinities are marginalized and subordinated. These men are not able to successfully align themselves with the dominant images due to, for example, racial, class, and sexuality barriers. While all men have some gender privilege, the key point is that not all men benefit equally from this system of privilege.

Within video games, black masculinity is most often stereotyped as hypermasculine, hyperphysical, and hypersexual. With this hyperextended black male, his character is mostly devoid of intellect and exists in a childlike, buffoon manner. The Gears of War nonplayable character Augustus "Cole Train" Cole reveals this reality. In the futuristic world of Sera where Gears of War takes place, much attention is paid to the details of the world, from the characters, to settings, to story line. However, in constructing the player of Cole Train, Epic Gamers reverts to common narratives associated with blackness and black masculinity.

Cole Train's character operates as comic relief often. This lack of maturity for military personnel reflects a common story often told of black sidekicks in movies, television, and video games. Analyzing representations of black men in this manner reveals that the predominate images depict them as a hybrid of "Coon" or "Black Buffoon," commonly referred to in media analysis as the Uncle Remus. The pure "Coon" is a stumbling, stuttering idiot, is often defined as unreliable, has limited mastery of English language, and lacks intelligence. The Uncle Remus is considered a hybrid of coon because of his stupidity, naiveté, and loyalty to his white counterparts. This type of character is used merely to elicit laughter evoking from exploited, exaggerated, and racialized stereotypes (Leonard, 2006). Cole Train's character, often providing comic relief, reflects this imagery. Throughout the gameplay, he is often heard saying very "jive" -like comments that show his lack of seriousness in the midst of warfare. His comments and ad libs commonly reflect what is known as "jive," or rather a highly stereotypical assessment of black vernacular made popular through media. Jive was a manner of speaking in code for black Americans so whites would not understand what they were saying. Jive has evolved into modern day Ebonics, slang and urban vernaculars. When alternative vernacular is incorporated into popular media, it is highly stereotyped and fetishized. It renders the bearer of the speech ignorant and incapable of serious thought and agency. Jive and other alternative forms of speech for blacks were a form of protest, defense mechanisms, and methods of deriving pleasure from something those not familiar with the language would be unable to understand. Popular culture's adoption of black vernacular into characters adds to the marketing appeal of "commodified ghetto cool." As will be discussed in later chapters, this co-opting of culture is a means to reduce and simplify black characters, making them appear ignorant. This racialization of characters is a common practice not only in video games, but in movies, TV, and news as well. This particular discourse serves "dominant actors to maintain domination" (Germond-Duret, 2012, p. 138), or in this case, black masculinity is shown as inferior to white masculinity, confirming and sustaining its domination as the example of Cole Train reveals.

1.3 CONCLUSION

The examples presented in this chapter reflect the video game industry's penchant for deploying ideologies from a hegemonic standpoint. The ideological projects deployed in the examples illustrate race and gender in stereotypical terms. This devaluing of certain populations only confirms their marginalized status within gaming, technology, and society in general. As Omi and Winant (1994) suggest in discussing race as an ideological project, it is not a physical or biological reality. Rather, race is created under conditions of power whereby historically, one group dominates others politically, economically, and socially. A racial project is then how race is used under conditions of power brokerage, whereby hegemony operates the allocation and compliance with the distribution of power. Through this theoretical framework, race forms through groups' use of race as a political platform, and the use of power for groups to be dominant and/or subordinate other groups. Omi and Winant (1994, p. 59) describe a racial project as "simultaneously an interpretation, representation, or explanation of racial dynamics, and an effort to reorganize and redistribute resources along particular racial lines." So race becomes common sense—a way of comprehending, explaining, and acting in the world. Video games as racial projects tell a story about certain groups from a hegemonic standpoint. The meaning attached to the characters of Augustus Cole, CJ, from San Andreas, and Lara Croft, among others, narrates a particular story of certain bodies within a larger social structure. Narrating race and gender in this manner generates certain ontological effects at the individual, institutional, and societal level. It tells a story, a singular story about black inner-city life, about women as heroes, and about masculinity in the military. These singular narratives skew the realities of diverse bodies and are dangerous because they are so powerful and it is difficult to recognize their power.

CHAPTER 2

Racing and Gendering the Game

Young Lara is curious, excited, and ambitious. She records every intriguing moment as a young adventurer would. She collects supplies that she stumbles upon not knowing when each item might come in handy leading to her eventual survival or defeat. Her thought process is interrupted by screams from familiar lungs. This shrieking sound is followed by the barks from what sounds like packs of wolves closing in on her friend, mentor, and adventure mate. When she approaches Roth, he is badly injured but the wolves have dissipated. She quickly reacts tending to his injuries. Roth informs her that the wolves have taken off with a food pack that also contained their medical supplies and other viable tools needed for survival in the wild — including a transmitter which is their way off the island to get Roth the much needed medical attention. Consumed by pain, shock, and fear, Roth passes out leaving young Lara to fend for herself. With no other options, Lara quickly dismisses her fears and panic, and with extreme courage, she locates the path created by the fleeing wolves and embarks on a journey to retrieve the looted goods.

This excerpt is a common theme throughout the Lara Croft Tomb Raider series. The young Lara oftentimes finds herself stranded on her own, having to toil through treacherous terrain, encountering foes of all shapes and sizes. Of course, this is a common story line for most heroes, whether in movies or in video games. But what makes Lara Croft so compelling is that she is one of the highest grossing video game characters and franchises in history. And she has done it all with female anatomy.

Heroines are few within video games. As this book will illustrate, most female characters within video games are highly stereotypical. Although Miss Croft is not without her hypersexualized flaws, as subsequent chapters will illustrate, she represents a successful incorporation of women into the dominant narrative so often held by male counterparts. Lara Croft still exists as a token, one among too many male heroes. For more women to be successfully blended into the dominant narratives held by men, there would need to be a complete ideological paradigm shift in how women are viewed not only within the video gaming industry, but in popular culture as well. Thus far, women are objectified and only illustrated through a singular lens. The following example provides a descriptive overview of the value of women when incorporated into the hegemonic world of video games.

> *The location is Banoi. The task is survive. Zombies have overtaken a once-beautiful island and they are terrorizing a small group immune from infection. Former football player Logan Carter, struggling rapper Sam B, island waitress Xian Mei, and ex-police officer Purna have survived a first wave, only to learn that the zombie infection, the Kuru strain, has spread and they must continue fighting. A secret group operating on the island reveal that the zombie-creating virus was created as a possible weapon. The group learns more about the secret behind this virus that was intentionally released to test its effect on humans. The group of immune are a threat to this secret and they are chased by not only the zombies, but by the corrupt government and military officials.*

The above excerpt is not a novel story, especially in the realm of zombie stories. What makes this story novel is its incorporation of a diverse cast of heroes. One hero in particular, Purna Jackson, is a black female whose skills and abilities can potentially outmatch any male she encounters. Within the game, a specific unlockable skill has been created just for her and it allows her to inflict more damage against male victims. Although this skill is called "Gender Wars" within the game, its original name was "Feminist Whore." This buried code was discovered by a computer gamer when a nonretail version of the game was accidentally sent to a digital game store (Crecente, 2011). Why is this significant to the study of race and gender in video games? This single example highlights hegemonic masculinity, female objectification, the intersection of race and gender, and the continued subordination of women within the video gaming industry. The game developer, Techland, apologized and situated the actions within the behavior of one individual.

> "It has come to our attention that one of Dead Island's leftover debug files contains a highly inappropriate internal script name of one of the character skills. This has been inexcusably overlooked and released with the game," Blazej Krakowiak, Techland International Brand Manager, said via email. "The line in question was something a programmer considered a private joke. The skill naturally has a completely different in-game name and the script reference was also changed. What is left is a part of an obscure debug function. This is merely an explanation but by no means an excuse. In the end that code was made a part of the product and signed with our company name. We deeply regret that fact and we apologize to all our customers or anyone who might have been offended by that inappropriate expression ... The person responsible for this unfortunate situation will

face professional consequences for violating the professional standards
and beliefs Techland stands for."

(Crecente, 2011, para. 6)

The comments posted in response to this article highlight the contentious relationship between women and an industry that continues to cater to males. Summarizing one commenter, the problem is a general trend in gaming that disrespects women and views women as some kind of enemy. There is a lack of seriousness devoted to examples like these.

As was discussed earlier, hegemonic masculinity is understood as the pattern of practices that allow men's dominance over women (Connell & Messerschmidt, 2005). As opposed to looking specifically at masculinity, hegemonic masculinity explains the construction of masculinity as a process, not simply as a set of expectations or an identity. Hegemonic masculinity should be explored as a pattern of practices that continue to objectify women and situate them in a continual state of subordination. As the example from Dead Island reveals, this female objectification constitutes an historical process in excluding and discrediting women. Hegemonic masculinity is an active process explaining how men play an active role and are often constrained by a limited set of choices in an all-male setting such as the video gaming industry. It makes it difficult for men to act in ways that can dismantle female subordination. This hegemonic collective is deeply embedded in our structure; we normalize it and it operates under a common sense notion. At some point, some individual who did not buy into this structure should have said, "maybe referring to a woman with super powers as a feminist whore is not the best idea." That did not happen.

Many game developers suggest that no offense is intended when women and people of color are stereotyped or disrespected in some manner within the video gaming industry. These examples are consumed and then discussed in isolated terms and are not viewed within the larger industry. Exploring video games within the larger framework of masculinity and whiteness would allow us to then situate them within these hegemonic frameworks that are telling a story, a single story (albeit complex?) of women or of ethnic minorities. Several examples have been provided to help illustrate the singular, stereotypical narrative told of women and minorities, but we must look broader. We must begin to look at a variety of video games to explore the extent of the problem.

2.1 THE WHITE MESSIAH IN THE SHOOTER

Although video games are works of fiction, they are constructed in a manner that makes them believable by portraying things and persons we recognize because of their likeness to elements in our social environment. As Vera and Gordon (2003) suggest, these social representations make sense to us because of the ideas and experiences we share with those involved in creating the art. What is being presented is not just entertainment as many would like to suggest. The stories told of certain people, places, and things make them very effective producers of certain ideology, and if presented in any other manner, they would be quickly dismissed. As Denzin (1995) posits, we live in a cinematic society and the portrayals set forth are important because it reflects in part, our actual society. Video games are largely a replica of the Hollywood blockbuster template so it is not shocking to find that the majority of video game protagonists are white and male.

A common narrative is of a white hero triumphing over physically powerful nonwhites through his physically ability, superior intellect, command of technology, and emotional control (as cited in Brock, 2011). Marcus Fenix from the Gears of War franchise exemplifies this common story told of the white hero. Marcus Fenix could be viewed as synonymous with the action hero from popular movies, the messiah who ultimately saves the day. There are many common traits associated with the "White Messiah" with popular media. He often sacrifices himself to save oppressed people. Marcus Fenix, as a leader of the Coalition of Ordered Government Army (COG) army, leads his soldiers in battle to defeat the enemy that has destroyed his world. The Messiah is often treated like royalty or a god and is instantly worshipped (Vera & Gordon, 2003). By traveling from place to place within the world of *Sera*, Marcus Fenix becomes a legend among the survivors. He also has much charisma, a quality that legitimizes his role as leader and savior of his darker-skinned followers. This very much reflects the reality of Gears of War. Marcus' sidekicks of color include Cole (a black male), Dom (a Latino male), Tai (an indigenous character based on the New Zealand Maori), and Kim (an Asian-American male). Just to note, there are white companions to Marcus (Baird, Carmine, and others), and there is even a female companion (Anya). As has been noted, the characters of color are racialized, and Anya even serves as Marcus' love interest, which is very problematic and will be discussed at length later in the text.

Dom's character greatly reflects the stereotypical Latin lover because of his constant concern for his wife Maria, who ultimately dies within the story. Tai's indigenous character is illustrated throughout the story line. His meditative personality is always discussed as well as references to his warrior—philosopher upbringing. He is also the only COG to ever discuss religion or spirituality in any manner. Kim's character is marked by extreme structure, being referred to often as "by the book." He once expressed disappointment at an abandoned school, hinting at the stereotype of the smart Asian. I provide these examples first, to show that some games have successfully incorporated characters of color. Unfortunately, these examples reflect the narrative so commonly told of people of color.

Returning to Marcus as the White Messiah, his character succeeds against impossible odds against villains saving town after town within *Sera*. An analysis of action heroes in movies, this is a reflection of American civic religions, "which transforms collective endeavors into the battle of a lone individual against the forces of organized evil" (Vera & Gordon, 2003, p. 116). This type of white action messiah reaffirms the fantasy of an autonomous individual. Although historically the action hero is typically a loner, in examples such as Gears of War, the messiah brings with him a multicultural team of helpers, also commonly seen in movies. They sacrifice themselves at their own expense by being loyal servants to their hero.

2.2 RACIALIZED REPRESENTATIONS WITHIN OTHER GENRES

Outside of the shooter genre, cultural representations are still stereotyped. Given the growing popularity of many games within this genre, and also their inclusion of an increased number of racial minorities, it is an area that needs to be examined for their depictions. As Leonard reveals, eight out of ten black male video game characters are situated within sports games. As in the larger society, black males find increased representation and visibility within the sporting world although largely limited and still controlled (Leonard, 2004). The black characters within these games, however, are much more likely to display aggressive behaviors such as trash talking and pushing than their white counterparts (Leonard, 2003). By situating blackness within this hypermasculine manner, it continues to narrate the ideology of what constitutes black masculinity—as something physically dangerous (Davis, 1983). In sports games such as NBA Street, Street Hoops, and NFL Street, they are situated in ghetto, urban locations and set to hip-hop soundtracks, "thereby staging a convergence of discourses on athleticism, blackness, and commodified ghetto cool" (Chan, 2005, p. 27). Situating black characters within these settings is confirming what hegemonic ideology so often deploys of black reality in the United States. As David Leonard discusses,

> The popularity of the game has less to do with its game playability, but its emphasis on an imagined street (black) culture. Whether the never-ending hip-hop soundtrack or the numerous shots of graffiti art, the game plays America's love affair with urban America, particularly that which is imagined as black. As games glamorize inner city spaces, commodifying them seedy and dangerous places, structural shifts continue to worsen these spaces of life. Reflecting the hyper-visibility and glorification of deindustrialized inner city community, games like NFL Street and Street Hopes reflect the commodification of African American practices of play within popular culture.
>
> (Leonard, 2004, p. 3)

Outside of the sports genre, racial depictions in video games are even more pronounced. For instance, True Crime is an action—adventure series that has featured an Asian-American and African-American lead character. In the first installment of True Crime, lead character Nick Kang is an officer with the Los Angeles Police Department and is essentially a bad cop. The game's stereotypical imagery is deployed most vividly in Kang's orientalism in that it is highly "fetishized and demonized" (Chan, 2005, p. 29). Additionally, the Asian culture of Los Angeles is "othered" providing a virtual tour of Chinatown—from the hegemonic standpoint (Gray, 2011).

By using Stuart Hall's definition of representation, we can begin to understand how problematic these depictions are. He broadly defines representation as the process by which members of a culture use a signifying system to produce and reproduce meaning and value (Hall, 1997, p. 61). The discourse attached to the meanings of "Asian-ness" enables the dominant to classify, control, and naturalize certain knowledge as the "truth" and at the same time grants the dominant power over the subordinate, who do not possess such knowledge. Gaming audiences who consume the images and stories attached to this racialized narrative begin to associate the mediated content with the real world. By being constantly inundated with these common narratives, the audience is lead to believe these stories, which simplify the complexities of culture.

The stereotypical markers of Asian culture follow in the tradition of orientalism as discussed by Said (1978). The discourse of orientalism is situated between the differences of latent and manifest orientalism. Manifest orientalism changes from writer to writer but latent orientalism remains stable and constant. Yegenoglu (1998, p. 23) elaborates,

> Orientalism, then, simultaneously refers to the production of a systematic knowledge and to the site of the unconscious - desires and fantasies; it signifies how the 'Orient' is at once an object of knowledge and an object of desire.
> (Yu, 2004, p. 68)

Moreover, she claims that latent orientalism has fundamental significance and "wider implications than Said himself recognizes" because it is permanent and consistent (p. 23). Latent orientalism is useful in examining Asian culture as told through media outlets such as video games. We can refer to the imagery within video games as latent orientalist imagery—something unconscious that is still with us as a culture.

Gramsci explains that a hegemonic struggle exists when the dominant try to incorporate their world images into the subordinated ways of thinking. The struggle arises when the subordinated resist being incorporated (Gramsci, 1971). He regards the representation not only as a relationship between the dominant and the subordinated but also as a contested terrain without any guarantees of power. He stresses human agency, which may allow resistance from the margins in existing power relations. He observes that people decode, or "read," representation through their own knowledge and values, which do not necessarily correspond to those of the dominant (Hall, 1980). While focusing on "nonnecessary correspondence" between the encoding and decoding of representation, he argues that representation is more or less interpreted through people's particular ways of life, and thus their own cultures, which do not necessarily correspond to the dominant culture. Unfortunately, many media audiences have limited exposure to racial and ethnic minorities; furthermore, when those in positions of power and domination script a certain narrative for the subordinate on a consistent basis, that scripted story becomes true.

In the second installment of *True Crime*, African-American lead character Marcus Reed starts off stereotypically as a gang member but ultimately becomes a cop in the New York Police Department. However, he soon turns rogue as the game requires him to avenge the death of the man who saved him from the streets. Violence is normalized in Reed's life as the only option within the black community—from street violence (gangs) to state-sanctioned violence (police). Again, this example reveals the continued reference of violence to black life in the United States.

Returning to Grand Theft Auto, this popular video game has been discussed at length within academia and popular culture as well. However, Leonard (2003) rightly points out that critical discussions associated with stereotypical racial imagery have been overshadowed by discussions of violence and visual imagery of women. Although both are important to discuss, given youth are consumers of this media, the absence of race from these conversations is disturbing.

Just to provide a description of the racial landscape of Grand Theft Auto III, almost all of the innocent citizens in the fictional Liberty City are white, and "the police are White and paragons of virtue" (Leonard, 2003, p. 3).

> You, as the only White character, are sent to Liberty City to lead and/or control the other ... you accept jobs ranging from driving the "girls" (all of whom are prostitutes) to assassinating rival gang members (all people of color). Your enemies in Liberty City consist of a number of gangs: the Triads (Chinese); Yazuka (Japanese); Diablos ("Hispanic street gang"); South Side Hoods (blacks); the Columbian Cartel; and the Yardies (Jamaican).
>
> (Leonard, 2003, p. 3)

Grand Theft Auto, as a racial project, "legitimizes White supremacy and patriarchy and privileges whiteness and maleness" (p. 3). In this sense, white hegemony is legitimized through the process of othering and "pixelated minstrelsy" by depicting racial minorities singularly (Chan, 2005). The danger of this "single story," as author Adichie (2009) explains, is not that it is inaccurate, but rather that this narrow account is the only one visible, situating it as the only possible narrative (Gray, 2011).

A subsequent installment of Grand Theft Auto was located in the fictional city of San Andreas and resembles 1990s South Central, Los Angeles. Similar to the previous installment of GTA, discussions surrounding this game immediately centered on violent inner city life.

Few scholars note the extreme depictions of blackness and hypermasculinity in lead character Carl Johnson (CJ). For instance, CJ must constantly work out to avoid getting fat as he must maintain his muscular, masculine physique and uphold the "gangsta" lifestyle (Barrett, 2006, p. 96). Just as the sports genre focuses on the hypermasculine, hyperphysical body of the black male, these same images are present within other genres. This extreme focus on the black body removes the association between blackness and intellect, affirming the hegemonic narratives attached to the black body. As Paul Gilroy states,

> ...associating blackness with intelligence, reason and the activities of the mind challenges the basic assumptions of raciology [...] whereas giving "The Negro" the gift of the devalued body does not, even if that body is to be admired (as cited in Barrett, 2006, p. 97).

As Barrett (2006) explains, CJ becomes a black body being controlled by an external force and is not able to represent himself. Although this is the purpose of video games, to be in control, it reinforces hegemonic representations of "black bodies as disposable ... constructed as non-persons" (p. 98). So it becomes an extension of the criminal black male deployed in other media outlets (Gray, 2011).

An additional theme present in San Andreas is the reality in which you begin (CJ begins) the game. He lives in a "pseudo-shantytown ... under a bridge"; his "friends are all unemployed, parentless gangbangers" (Barrett, 2006, p. 101), and the violence in his life is immediate, automatic, and ever present (Gray, 2011). By not providing any explanation of these events, it reifies black inner-city life, totally ignoring structural inequality forces at work that have assisted in creating this reality—it is naturalized.

> Issues such as three-strikes laws, the vast and disproportionate increase in the imprisonment of African Americans since the early 1980s, the impact of neoliberal economic and social 'reform,' or the collapsing of public concerns into private interests are completely ignored. In place of a consideration of larger social causes, one is left to imagine that either this violent, unemployable, pathological behavior is the permanent, natural state of African Americans, or that somehow CJ and his friends have found themselves in this situation as a result of their own individual failings.
> (Barrett, 2006, p. 101)

Additionally, by situating people of color in these marginalized communities and whites in affluent suburbs, video games have once again succeeded in affirming the hegemonic status quo. This singular narrative continues the same mediated story so often deployed about blacks in America.

2.3 HEGEMONIC IMAGERY IN FIGHTING GENRES

This hegemonic imagery is present in fighting genres as well. For instance, Street Fighter, a popular series, has always featured stereotypical characters associated with particular countries. For instance, Blanka is a hulk-looking beast from Brazil, Guile is a hypermasculine American G.I., E. Honda is a sumo wrestler from Japan, El Fuerte is a Mexican character in search of spicy food, and Zangief is a Russian wrestler, just to name a few (Ware, 2010). Although Street Fighter is a Japanese game, race and culture are still stereotyped and deployed in a "comical and exaggerated" manner (p. 55). Importantly, in creating their own depictions of Asian-ness, there is no "primitiveness" in these characters of the sort that is usually indicative of Orientalism— Edward Said's process by which white Western discourse produces Eastern subjects as "savage" and "exotic" (p. 57). The American characters are hypermasculine and represent the Stallone, Van Damme, and Schwarzenegger types of characters. Similar to American video games, the elite power structures, creates, and deploys constructed images that perpetuate hegemonic structures of whiteness and masculinity. This is made obvious in Street Fighter's representation of second- and third-world characters. As Ware (2010) explains, this "Monstrous Other" is not associated with the Us (Asian East) or You (American West). In this sense, Japanese game designers have constructed and sustained white Western thinking of the default racial setting.

> Much of the reassertion of Japanese homogeneity shares a distinctly White Western ideology. ... This selling of the Other (necessarily Monstrous in Street Fighter, due to the exaggerated nature of the genre) creates an Other that is neither East Asian nor White Western; as game objects that are both playable (thus, controllable) and destructible (thus, marginalized).
>
> (Ware, 2010, p. 68)

In addition to the previously mentioned Blanka and Zangief, other "Monstrous Other" characters include: Dhalsim the Indian yogi, T. Hawk the Native American tribal chief, Dee Jay the Jamaican musician, Balrog the African-American boxer, Sagat the Thai kickboxer, M. Bison the third-world despot, and Akuma the otherworldly martial arts master (Ware, 2010, p. 69). Visually, these characters are drastically different, being abnormally tall, big, and often appearing almost animal-like, as in the case of Blanka, the Brazilian beast. The term "pixilated minstrelsy" (Chan, 2005) is appropriate in understanding the deployment of race and racialization in these genres in that race, racial imagery, and identity depicted in this manner lead to the deployment of hegemonic whiteness and masculinity. As Leonard (2003, pp. 1–2) explains,

> Race matters in the construction and deployment of stereotypes, and it matters in legitimizing widely accepted racial cues and assumptions both in the workplace and in leisure pursuits. In short, race matters in video games because many of them affirm the status quo, giving consent to racial inequality and the unequal distribution of resources and privileges.

2.4 GENDERED DEPICTIONS WITHIN VIDEO GAMES

Another problematic example of mediated portrayals of minorities in video games is through the popular franchise *Resident Evil 5* (RE5). RE5 revolves around an investigation of a terrorist threat in a fictional region in Africa. This game was mired within controversy given that the protagonist was charged with killing black zombie enemies in this village. There have been questions surrounding whether or not the imagery was in fact racist. Critics of the game express concerns that the game operated off the traditional media trope of the dangerous Dark Continent.

The companion to the white male protagonist (Chris) is a light-skinned black female (Sheva), which adds to the controversy. As Brock (2011) explains, the relationship between the duo confirms hegemonic control over the gendered and racialized other. Sheva's character is rendered invisible in the narrative as well as in the actual game play. Reducing the black female in this manner reduces her importance and agency within a story riddled with problems for its depiction of blackness as an enemy other. Sheva's character is also highly sexualized, given she is barely clothed throughout the game.

Sheva, as our guide through the Dark Continent, is far removed from African culture and she is unable to interact with Africans in the game. Although this is mostly the fault of the game not allowing for this engagement, it wasn't thought to include in the game. Capcom did not use Sheva's backstory to involve her character more deeply into the narrative (Brock, 2011). As Brock explains, "Sheva is the video-game equivalent of Pocahontas: a woman of color coerced into "guiding" White explorers across a foreign land that she is presumed to be familiar with because of her ethnic heritage" (p. 440). Her limited presence, sexual objectification, and exoticism all reinforce hegemonic notions of the female of color.

As has been previously discussed, the popular third-person shooter game Gears of War also stereotypically "others" women and people of color. Aside from the hyperphysical, hypermasculine, and hypersexual depictions of men of color within the game, this game celebrates mas-culinity and virtually excludes femininity. For instance, the only female character in the first installment of Gears of War, Anya Stroud,

> ...is a lieutenant—but you'd never know it, since the petite blond spends the game getting in and out of helicopters, narrowly escaping danger (off-screen, of course), and staying out of the real action while advising male soldiers over her headset. She must have been a heavily armored COG at some point, in order to move through the ranks—but if that's the case, where are all of the other female COGs.
>
> (Myers, 2010)

Although the third installment of Gears of War added Anya as a playable character, in addition to other females, she is not stereotypical as one would assume. Her body measurements are average. However, Anya's character is the sexual love interest to the protagonist, Marcus Fenix.

The Bechdel Test is useful in evaluating the roles that women have within video games. It was introduced in Alison Bechdel's comic strip *Dykes to Watch Out For.* In a 1985 comic strip titled "The Rule," a female character says that she only watches a movie if it satisfies the following requirements: (1) it has to have at least two women in it; (2) the women talk to each other; (3) the women must talk about some-thing besides a man. Although it was originally used to evaluate films, it's appropriate in examining other types of media as well including video games. Although Gears of War has yet to pass the Bechdel Test, among other video games, the latest installment of Lara Croft Tomb Raider actually comes close. As Pinchefsky (2013, pp. 1–2) explains in her Feminist Review of Tomb Raider, Lara converses with two women about survival.

The first woman, Sam Nishimura, is Lara's friend and roommate, and we see them first interact in a videotaped conversation. Sam, a filmmaker, is encouraging Lara to have more confidence in herself. Their subsequent conversations have nothing to do with men—only survival. The second woman, Joslin Reyes, is clearly hostile to Lara. It seems that the inexperienced Lara is the reason Reyes and her crew are on this disastrous mission, and she blames Lara for their troubles. Eventually Reyes comes to respect Lara.

A more dangerous theme prominent in how women are depicted in video games is centered on their sexual victimization. For instance, 90% of African-American women within console video games were victims of violence compared to 45% of white women (as cited in Leonard, 2003, p. 2). Even more disturbing, the sole function of the majority of the women within the video games is to perform sexual acts. A video game that highlights both of these examples is Grand Theft Auto. To provide an overview, female characters of color within GTA are prostitutes. They serve a functional purpose to the lead character in that they can improve overall health, extending your life. A sexual encounter with a prostitute raises your health. However, this is a paid service and once the encounter is complete, you have the option of killing her to get your money back (Leonard, 2003, p. 4). Unfortunately, much of the scholarship related to women and video games is associated with the visualization of women on magazine and video game covers. These hypersexualized depictions are reflective of the male gaze of the female body. As Mulvey articulates in her landmark article, this production of the male gaze situates the female body as the bearer of meaning, not maker of meaning (as cited in Kennedy, 2002). Similarly, Collins (1998) argues, the racialized female body is practically silenced when she is written into the narrative by hegemonic structures and remains powerless to speak for herself.

Although these studies are not reflective of actual game content, they are useful in understanding how women are incorporated into mainstream games. For instance, in their examination of video game covers, Burgess, Stermer, and Burgess (2007) found that males were portrayed four times more frequently than their female counterparts and females were depicted in a hypersexualized manner. In video game magazine articles, Miller and Summer (2007) similarly found that males were more likely to be shown as heroes while females were more likely to be portrayed in support roles. Dill and Thill (2007) also found that males were shown as more aggressive and females were shown more sexualized.

Returning to actual examples that discuss women's roles in video games, Lara Croft is an interesting case that simultaneously affirms and rejects hegemonic notions of whiteness and masculinity. Lara Croft's original character was a South American woman named Laura Cruz (McLaughlin, 2008). However, this name was not UK friendly enough and the change was made to whiten her character (the story line was also altered to incorporate a British origin). This omission of race affirms whiteness as the default setting inside gaming spaces (although originally she rejected whiteness). Additionally, she rejects hegemonic notions of masculinity by recreating the typical narrative of the male hero. Traditionally, the hero is male, and the females constitute supporting roles (Kennedy, 2002). However, her sexuality and disproportionate breasts were used to market her in addition to her physical abilities. In their content analysis of introductory films of video games, Jansz and Martis (2007) observed that breasts and buttocks were prominent features and seemed significant in marketing a video game. Using Mulvey's (1975) discussion on women in film narratives, Kennedy (2002) explains,

> ...that the female body operates as an eroticized object of the male gaze and the fetishistic and scopophilic pleasures which this provides for the male viewer. The ... "active" or "strong" female characters signify a potential threat to the masculine order (as cited in Kennedy, 2002, para. 8).

Downs and Smith (2009) identified this trend in their study of video game characters, finding that women were more likely to show partial nudity, have unrealistic body images (large breast/small waist), and wear sexually revealing clothing. Beasley and Standley (2002) also found this sex bias in how males were featured compared to females. Despite the increase in lead female characters in video games (Jansz & Martis, 2007), they are still depicted in stereotypical manners.

2.5 CONCLUSION

When discussions of cultural representations within video games arise, many suggest that as a form of entertainment, it doesn't matter. This mere idea diminishes the argument so commonly given when people consider media as just entertainment, reducing the seriousness of their imagery. Others suggest that this lack of true diverse engagement is purposefully given in belief that mainstream audiences are unable to relate to minority characters.

It is no accident that these games are being created with stereotypical imagery. Games are created based on the biases and opinions of their creators although video game developers contend no offense is intended. They suggest that their games are "simply parodies or a reflection of a sort of "browning" of popular culture that transcends race and sells to all in a marketplace captivated by hip-hop styles, themes, and attitudes" (Marriott, 2004). This exploitation of Asianness, blackness and hip-hop, and women still creates the single narrative of "other" life because there are few, if any, other images deployed in video games. On the other hand, whiteness is often depicted in an opposing manner with multiple narratives. This hegemonic vision of masculinity and whiteness only exists in relation to other forms of masculinity and femininity, allowing for the dominant—white male—to construct himself in a certain way, hence the continued othering of women and people of color in video games (Bucholz, 1999, p. 445).

PART II

The Gaming Space

CHAPTER 3

Deviant Acts: Racism and Sexism in Virtual Gaming Communities

This chapter will discuss the deviant acts of racism and sexism and the process that leads to these acts in virtual gaming communities. In the broad sense, deviance is a term that refers to behavior that does not conform to socially accepted norms established by rules. Deviance exists because social groups react in a condemnatory, punitive, or simply disapproving manner to any individual's behavior(s) and/or characteristic(s) that are in violation of the social standards prevailing in those groups (Clinard & Meier, 1998, p. 7). Because the Xbox Live space allows for real-time voice communication, much of the racism and sexism that emerge stem from linguistic profiling. Similar to racial profiling, linguistic profiling occurs when auditory cues as opposed to visual cues are used to confirm and/or speculate on the racial background of an individual (Baugh, 2003). Much of these acts of racism and sexism stem from the anonymous nature of virtual communities. As Suler and Phillips (1998) explain, anonymity on the Internet disinhibits people, compelling some to say and do things that they wouldn't otherwise say and do. And as previous studies have found, there is a process that emerges that leads to racist speech after linguistic profiling occurs: questioning, provoking, instigating, and ultimately racism. And as I contend, these acts should be viewed as deviant within the space.

3.1 DEVIANT BEHAVIOR IN VIRTUAL COMMUNITIES

In the broad sense, deviance is a term that refers to behavior that does not conform to socially accepted norms. Traditional definitions of deviance can be viewed from two opposing perspectives: either absolutist or relativist. In determining the level of deviance from the absolutist approach, sociologists and criminologists usually compare the degree of difference between the deviant behavior and the established norm, or as Newman (2008) suggests, absolutism views human behavior as "inherently proper and good" or "improper, immoral, evil, and bad" (p. 220). The problem with this approach is that there are arbitrary differences in right or wrong, especially when incorporating gender, race, class, age, and other factors. Social constructionists recognize that behaviors attached to particular groups of people, most notably marginalized populations, are deemed deviance and violating mainstream norms. There is also strong emotional reaction toward those considered deviant from the absolutist perspective as is often seen with the issue of same-sex marriage (Newman, 2008). This perspective mirrors a failure to conform notion and has led to strict social controls over behavior—the law and order effect. To increase social control, three things usually occur: (1) more rules are established, (2) these rules are strict and inflexible (for certain bodies), and (3) a system is put in place to punish violators (Gray, 2011). When this absolutist approach is adopted by social institutions, we see more laws and regulations prohibiting certain actions for certain people (Newman, 2008).

On the other hand, the relativist approach views that no behavior or person is inherently deviant; deviance emerges through a labeling process where some behaviors are identified as bad, undesirable, or unacceptable on the basis of rules made by those in positions of power (Coakley, 1994). For those who lack power within any social structure, their behavior may be labeled deviant more often than those with power. Relativist definitions of deviance recognize how many acts of deviance have been socially constructed and created based on "collective of human judgments and ideas" (Newman, 2008, p. 222). Powerless individuals don't have the resources to resist the deviant label when their behavior does not conform to the standards of the hegemonic structure. Most often, the aforementioned responses to social control occur in this instance as well. Throughout this text, deviance will be examined from the relativist approach exploring three distinct characteristics: (1) deviant behavior violates social norms in a particular space and results in punitive actions by those who established the norm, (2) one only becomes deviant or a behavior only becomes deviant once a negative valuation is placed on it, and (3) definitions of deviance vary based on the setting and the people around. This approach to deviance is similar to that of cultural criminologists who look broadly at mythical and misleading imagery, constructions of gender, ethnicity, age, and new forms of social control (Ferrell & Websdale, 1996). Although much of their focus is still on criminal behavior, their work recognizes the importance of power, identity and difference, and how constructions of identity impact the response of hegemonic structures in place in society leading to social control within particular spaces. This concept of labeling certain bodies deviant will be explored in a subsequent chapter.

Although deviance is mostly a socially constructed concept, deviant behaviors in most real-world settings have been agreed upon by some level of consensus. In virtual settings, identifying deviant behavior is more difficult to determine. In the broad sense, deviance is a term that refers to behavior that does not conform to socially accepted norms established by rules. Even though terms of service and the code of conduct within Xbox Live prohibit the use of certain types of speech, racism and sexism included, individuals still engage in this behavior. To examine why a person might participate in this deviant behavior, an examination of player types needs to occur.

3.1.1 Types of Gamers in Virtual Communities

Deviance within virtual communities has been documented by scholars for years. For instance, Richard Bartle was one of the earliest scholars to provide a systematic overview of the killer, which is a type of user within a multiuser domain (MUD). A MUD is a multiplayer virtual world that operates in real time (Bartle, 1996). These virtual worlds are usually text based, but more contemporary and advanced MUDs are incorporating other types of communication, including voice chat. As this chapter will explain later, communication leads to much of the deviance that occurs within these virtual gaming spaces. But an examination of the different types of players and different styles of play is important to discuss.

Bartle's taxonomy of users in MUDs arose from a forum discussion among members within the forum. A question was posed asking users what their expectations were from a MUD and what they wanted to get out of interaction within the space (Bartle, 1996). Users responded in a variety of manners but themes and patterns did emerge regarding what they liked, what they didn't like, and what they would improve. By examining the content of their responses, Bartle organized the users in this particular MUD, grouping them into four distinct categories. These categories created one of the earliest taxonomies of gamers in virtual spaces. Bartle (1996) identified that most users enjoyed four aspects of MUDs: achievements gained within games, exploring the virtual world and experimenting with it, using communication features to socialize, and/or causing distress to other players (achiever, explorer, socializer, and killer) (Gray, 2011). Bartle and other scholars recognize that players may adhere to any number of categories at any time and that it largely depends on a player's mood, the type of game being played, or even the user's gaming style. Although this taxonomy has been expanded, it is still useful to see the basic motivations of gamers within online spaces. Within Xbox Live, gamers do exhibit all player styles, but it must be understood that much of it largely depends on the specific game (Gears of War, Call of Duty), game genre (shooter, driver, etc.), and player mood.

The player style that influences deviance the most within Xbox Live is the category of "killer." To reiterate, these players derive enjoyment by imposing themselves on others most often by player killing. As Bartle (1996) found, the more distress killers cause, the greater the killer's joy. The ability to engage in "overkill" varies by game as well. Games with unlimited lives or unlimited re-spawn (coming back to life after a kill) have the potential to exceed the limits of a killer's joy. Overkilling, senseless killing, or killing for enjoyment that fall outside the normal parameters of the games' intention can be referred to as griefing and has been discussed at length in the literature. Griefing has been defined as the intentional harassment of a player that falls outside normal gameplay (Foo & Koivisto, 2004; Lin & Sun, 2005; Myers, 2007; Smith, 2004; Warner & Raiter, 2005). Griefing can also be understood as a source of deep mental anguish, annoyance, or frustration that one player experiences at the hands of another player (as cited in Foo & Koivisto, 2004). Grief players are considered deviant because they intentionally violate codes, rules, and overall appropriate gaming etiquette of the virtual gaming communities in which they are interacting.

3.1.2 Griefing

It is important to distinguish that a player who engages in griefing behavior derives his or her enjoyment not from actually playing the game as the game developer intended, but rather from causing other gamers to become distracted and annoyed during gameplay. An example from outside of the Xbox Live context looks at this phenomena. In World of Warcraft, a popular Massively Multiplayer Online Role Playing Game (MMORPG), there is a spell that is powerful enough to kill lower level characters almost instantly; when the characters of these players return to their respective towns, they spread this spell like a virus to new areas (Warner & Raiter, 2005). This intentional infection is a griefing tactic of which players who learn to modify the space take advantage. This was not the original intent of the game's developer. Another example from World of Warcraft that is actually seen in other virtual games is camping. Camping refers to killing players' characters immediately when they spawn back to life after a death or kill. Some killers who engage in killing for enjoyment organize their efforts that seriously undermine the scope of the game and the enjoyment of other players. The more organized the efforts, the more distracting it can be, seriously detracting from the overall enjoyment of the game, which is the original intention.

3.1.3 Flaming

Another concept that leads to acts of deviance in virtual gaming communities is known as flaming. Similar to griefing, flaming refers to negative antisocial behaviors, including the expression of hostility, the use of profanity, and the venting of strong emotions (Thompsen, 2003). Gamers who engage in flaming use outwardly hostile speech toward other gamers using text- or voice-based communication. This is the category which includes sexist, heterosexist, and racist speech and is the only definition that encompasses what gamers of color and women experience in Xbox Live. As Dorwick explains, flaming can be understood as the spontaneous creation of homophobic, racist, and misogynist language during electronic communication (cited in Thompsen, 2003). This definition is useful to explaining what occurs because of the incorporation of the word "spontaneous," because most of the hostile speech is unwarranted and comes out of nowhere.

3.2 ONLINE DISINHIBITION

The overt presence of racist, sexist, and heterosexist speech in online spaces was examined by Suler and Phillips (1998). They suggest that anonymity on the Internet disinhibits people, compelling some to say and do things that they wouldn't otherwise say or do. Because virtual spaces allow for a certain level of anonymity, people don't know who you are, and some users are compelled to say and do things that they wouldn't normally say face to face in physical spaces. But this online disinhibition can work in two ways—benign and toxic. Users who display benign disinhibition show unusual acts of kindness and generosity. On the other hand, toxic disinhibition occurs when users employ "rude language, harsh criticisms, anger, hatred, and even threats" (Suler, 2004, p. 321). There are six factors that characterize online disinhibition: (1) dissociative anonymity, (2) invisibility, (3) asynchro-nicity, (4) solipsistic introjections, (5) dissociative imagination, and (6) minimization of status and authority. By briefly describing each one, the realities of deviance within virtual gaming communities becomes apparent, allowing one to recognize how it is able to transpire.

3.2.1 Dissociative Anonymity

Dissociative anonymity refers to the ability to hide your identity in online spaces. Since anonymity is a principal factor leading to the disinhibition effect, users can separate their online actions from their real-world selves; whatever they say and/or do can't be linked to them in the real world in some cases. Some individuals may even justify their actions by convincing themselves that they aren't connected to the online persona at all. This is an important factor in explaining the deviant behavior of racism and sexism. Many users suggest that their racist and/or sexist behavior, among other types of hostile speech, is not serious and just a part of the trash talking nature of the virtual gaming community. This is a common explanation from hardcore gamers. And since many online environments allow users the opportu-nity to be invisible as they move in and out of web sites, message boards, and sometimes chat rooms, the seriousness of their actions are never met with consequences. This invisibility gives users the courage to say and do things they may not normally say and do. Within Xbox Live, the virtual community requires gamers to have a standing gamer-tag which allows a certain level of anonymity. This voice-based com-munity does require a certain level of disclosure for users who engage in voice-based communications. Others within the space can hear how others sound, revealing certain aspects of one's identity.

In some online spaces, an individual's identity may be known, but being "physically invisible amplifies the disinhibition effect" (Suler, 2004, p. 322). Avoiding eye contact and face-to-face interaction can sometimes lead to disinhibition. Within text-based communities, people don't have to worry about how they look or sound when they type a message. They don't have to worry about how others look or sound in response to what they say. Seeing a frown, a shaking head, a sigh, a bored expression, and many other subtle and not so subtle signs of disapproval or indifference can inhibit what people are willing to express (Suler, 2004). The incorpo-ration of emoticons has allowed some level of emotion within text-based communities. But again, in voice-based communities such as Xbox Live emotions have the ability to be more easily heard.

3.2.2 Asynchronicity

Asynchronicity is one factor that does not directly apply to Xbox Live but is important to examine when researching communication in virtual communities in general. Asynchronicity implies that communication does not occur in real time in online spaces. This is sometimes true in e-mail and message boards where it can take minutes, hours, days, or months for a reply, or even that long in sending. As Suler (2004) explains, not having to deal with someone's immediate reaction disinhibits people. In face-to-face, real-time, communications, the receiver of a message has the option to respond immediately. This reality restricts certain types of behaviors among individuals. For instance, individuals who don't like confrontations may restrict certain types of communications (angry, hostile, etc.).

In Xbox Live, there are multiple modes of communication employed. There is real-time voice chat, there is instant messaging, there are e-mail messages, and there is video chat, among others. From previous research conducted on communication in Xbox Live, users mostly employ real-time voice chat, or synchronous communication (Gray, 2011). But because of the relative invisibility, there is still a level of anonymity, leading many users to engage in toxic disinhibition.

3.2.3 Solipsistic Introjection

Solipsistic introjection implies that the lack of face-to-face cues or textual communication can alter self-boundaries (Suler, 2004). Face-to-face communications lead most of us to establish certain borders around communication so we only say or do certain things. This also means that we will create and fill in the blanks, if you will, certain aspects of one's identity or personality based on what is not revealed by that user. Restricting our own virtual persona gives others the empowered ability to create it for us. So if a user is restricting the use of voice in a voice-based community, a motivated user may decide to "create" a voice or imagine what the silent user sounds like. If a user has not created an avatar, other users may imagine what the user looks like (although some users opt for the avatar to bear no resemblance of the self). What essentially happens is the user who refuses to disclose all aspects of self runs the risk of having another person create a perceived reality for him or her.

of disinhibition is significant for many reasons. As Suler
s, cyberspace can become a stage where we are merely
er people's worlds. Leaving parts of our identity hidden
to create. What they create could be a diminished or inferior virtual persona and justify that person reacting in a condemnatory
manner (racist, sexist, etc.) without warrant or justification. So what
users may perceive to be a spontaneous act of racism may in fact be a
creation in that motivated user's mind (I think this person is black so
I'm going to defame them).

3.2.4 Dissociative Imagination

Dissociative imagination is a very important concept to examine in
understanding how acts of deviance, most notably racism and sexism,
occur in virtual gaming communities. This aspect of disinhibition
occurs when users make the mistake of assuming virtual worlds are
make-believe spaces. Many users in virtual spaces separate their virtual
lives from their offline, physical bodies, suggesting that their virtual
life is a game where the rules don't apply to real life (Suler, 2004). This
misunderstanding leads some users to engage in behavior that they
normally wouldn't in the real world. A user who employs this method
of disinhibition privileges physical interactions and devalues the real
nature of virtual spaces. This assumption can lead one to use vulgar
speech directed toward women and people of color, hoping that the
recipient also diminishes the importance of virtual interactions. From
what the research suggests, women and people of color take acts of
racism and sexism seriously in any space and virtual spaces are not
exempt from this view. The problem is that the motivated offender
relinquishes the responsibility for what happens in a so-called make-
believe play world that has nothing to do with reality (Suler, 2004).
The space is real and the people are real, and all interactions need to
be taken seriously. This dissociative imagination occurs more readily
in fantasy game environments where an imaginary character is played
by a user.

3.2.5 Minimization of Status and Authority

The last factor conceptualizing disinhibition refers to the minimization
of status and authority. This important tenet reflects the reality of
many virtual spaces, including gaming communities: the absence of a
suitable guardian supervising the space leads some users to engage in
deviant behaviors. As Suler (2004) explains, authority figures usually

express their status and power in their dress and body language and in the trappings of their environmental settings. So in virtual communities, the presence of an online moderator to facilitate interactions is evidence of an authority figure. However, the absence of traditional authoritarian cues reduces the impact of authority in digital spaces. Even when authority figures are known to users, the lack of physical presence and cues continues to diminish their power within the space.

In Xbox Live, there is usually no presence of an authority figure. When one does appear, it is usually when a complaint is filed, and this does not occur in every instance. In the first installment of Gears of War, it was rumored that a ghost character would appear in rooms to seek out possible hackers. But this has not been confirmed. But if it were in fact true, the presence of a ghost moderator to look for hackers is outside the scope of this tenet. This ghost authority was not interested in virtual communications, especially those that were racist or sexist in nature.

Within Xbox Live online forums, there is a moderator that ensures terms of service and code of conduct are upheld. But again, a posting in this text-based community of Xbox Live only appears when a conversation is flagged for review. Without the presence of an authority figure in virtual communities, people are disinhibited with the absence, leading them to speak out, misbehave, and engage in a deviant manner.

As research suggests, the greater the levels of anonymity in a virtual community, the greater the acts of deviance in these communities may be. But what occurs when anonymity is not a factor? What happens when users are able to hear how others sound? What happens when we can determine a person's race or gender without that person disclosing that information? This aspect of deviance will be explained in the next section.

3.3 LINGUISTIC PROFILING: THE ORIGIN OF DEVIANCE IN XBOX LIVE

When on the phone with a stranger, many Americans can guess that person's ethnic background and gender from the first hello (or many attempt to guess). But what often occurs is that many people make racist judgments about the person on the other end who may have a unique dialect. This type of profiling based on linguistic cues is what occurs in voice-based virtual communities daily.

Similar to racial profiling, linguistic profiling is based upon auditory cues that may include racial identification, but which can also be used to identify other linguistic subgroups within a given speech community (Baugh, 2003). Scholars have long studied linguistic stereotypes, finding discrimination based on accents and dialects against speakers of various ethnic backgrounds. What is seen in the American context is that voice discrimination and linguistic profiling is used as an effective means to filter out individuals who may be deemed inferior, leading one to not engage in meaningful relationships with this type of other. This kind of discrimination is more subtle and difficult to detect, especially in physical spaces. And other factors, aside from the voice-based discrimination, may be used to deny that person services. As Baugh (2003) found in his research on housing discrimination, individuals just rarely returned phone calls or respond to written correspondence.

Identifying one's racial identity based on speech captured the public's attention during the trial of O.J. Simpson. Simpson's attorney, Mr. Cochran, objected to the thought that someone could ascertain your racial identity based on how you sound. Additionally, a case in Kentucky employed linguistic profiling to convict an African-American appellant who was overheard by a white police officer (Baugh, 2003). This case affirmed the legality of racial identification based on speech by a lay witness (as cited in Gray, 2011).

Within the virtual world, Joinson (2001) suggests that the anonymous spaces of the Internet compel users to disclose personal information about themselves, knowing that the party on the other end will never find out their true identity. For example, if I were engaged in a conversation with someone and disclosed my occupation, the person on the other end would have no true way of confirming this information. Additionally, I could create a false identity altogether with no way of really knowing my true self and true identity. Physical identifiers are a bit different. In virtual, voice communities, some information that we might not normally disclose, such as our race or gender, can be automatically relayed in the space. So when a male gamer speaks through his headset, the gamers on the other end can immediately decipher his gender. When women speak, most often, gamers can ascertain the gender. Although race and other identities are not easily translated into virtual space, profiling still occurs to confirm one's identity.

It is true that some individuals can use outside modifications to alter the voice. The Xbox system does not come with these kinds of alterations or features. So the real voice can be heard. As many women and people of color explain, this mere technological advance creates the most havoc in their virtual lives—racial and gendered hatred based on how people sound. The next section goes into the process to actually explain how linguistic profiling may lead to racism. From what scholarship suggests about racism in Xbox Live, it follows a traditional format: questioning, provoking, instigating, racist speech, and either diffusion or a virtual race war.

3.4 THE PROCESS LEADING TO RACISM

Questioning is the first step that may lead to racism. The simple question asked is "are you black" attempting to confirm the sound of blackness. As illustrated in previous studies on Xbox Live, the majority of observed racist behaviors did in fact begin with this question or another similar racial inquiry. The second step in the process is provoking. This provoking takes the form of harassment similar to griefing. However, racism should be understood independent from flaming and griefing. The difference is that this harassment is always linked to the body, an aspect out of gamers' control (Gray, 2011). Returning to provoking, many gamers who used racist language recited offensive black and/or immigrant jokes, challenged the penis size of black men, challenged citizenship of Latino-sounding gamers, explained disgust for big lips, criticized the use of Ebonics, and even disrespected black mothers. The purpose of this provoking seemed to be a means to situate blackness as inferior, deeming it deviant within this space.

Most of the time the provoking would lead into instigation, but oftentimes instigating preceded provoking. Either way, instigation was the only step that sometimes would not occur. But when it did, gamers using this racist speech would enter a game room with friends and this group of friends would fuel the "flames" of the offending gamer. Oftentimes the friends will ad lib the statements of the offender or just joke and laugh at the comments made. This provoking and instigation leads to the ultimate act of racism, which is the black-sounding gamer being called "nigger." No matter what the previous responses of the gamer of color was, the offending gamer would eventually say "nigger."

Once this word was uttered, either diffusion or a virtual race war followed. If diffusion occurred, either the offending gamer or the gamer of color would leave or get removed from the game by the host of the gaming session. If there was no diffusion, then the black-sounding gamer would enter into a heated argument using profanity and racist language as well.

The racism and sexism that many gamers experience within Xbox Live is more than the harassment described by griefing and should not be replaced by the term flaming (Gray, 2011). The fact that racism and sexism have a historical context deems it more serious and it needs to be researched and studied separate from other antisocial behaviors. Importantly, the explanations offered on griefing and flaming do not seem to fully encapsulate what is witnessed in Xbox Live. The gamers who commit acts of racism and sexism are not viewed as deviant within the space. There is not a massive effort to restrict these individuals or punish them in any way, even with the feedback system in place. The victims of these acts essentially become the deviants for failing to conform to the norm of the default gamer. The next chapter explains this premise in more detail.

CHAPTER 4

Deviant Bodies: Racism, Sexism, and Intersecting Oppressions

Thus far, I have argued that video games and online gaming spaces deploy and maintain whiteness and masculinity as privilege. What results is linguistic profiling based on how these women and people of color sound, resulting in their marginalization. With this chapter, I will argue that marginalized gamers within Xbox Live have been constructed as deviant bodies, undeserving of the full status of gamer by the default white male. This chapter will give substance to these arguments through the experiences and perspectives of minority gamers. It is my hope that their stories and experiences will demonstrate how individual acts of racism, sexism, heterosexism, and other inequalities manifest in this online gaming community as well as how normalized these events have become to marginalized gamers experiencing them.

4.1 DEVIANT BODIES, RACISM, AND XBOX LIVE

Most of the time the provoking would lead into instigation, but oftentimes instigating preceded provoking. Either way, instigation was the only step that sometimes would not occur. But when it did, gamers using this racist speech would enter a game room with friends and this group of friends would fuel the "flames" of the offending gamer. Oftentimes, the friends will ad lib the statements of the offender or just joke and laugh at the comments made. This provoking and instigation leads to the ultimate act of racism, which is the black-sounding gamer being called "nigger." No matter what the previous responses of the gamer of color was, the offending gamer would eventually say "nigger." Once this word was uttered, either diffusion or a virtual race war followed. If diffusion occured, either the offending gamer or the gamer of color would leave or get removed from the game by the host. If there was no diffusion, then the black-sounding gamer would enter into a heated argument using profanity and racially insensitive language as well.

Listening to the chatter inside Xbox Live would not immediately evoke cause for concern. The gamers typically talk about strategy within the gaming space, coordinate flanks to overtake the other team, joke with one another, and have other general conversations. When the offending gamer enters the room, conversations change. When the default gamer hears the black-sounding gamer, he lashes out and eventually calls the black gamer "nigger." Within the interviews conducted, the black gamer was asked about lashing out in turn toward the white male gamer. His response was very telling, as the excerpt below reveals:

> Silentassassin321: Are you joking? I ain't hurtin' his feelings. What could I possibly say that would hurt this muh'fuckah. He white. Ain't shit I can say that will equal the word nigga.

His justification raises an interesting point. The term "nigger" seems to be the pinnacle of hate speech and when used toward this victimized gamer creates a great deal of emotional anguish that could lead to violence if he was able to locate this offender.

> Silentassassin321: If I could find this bitch I would whoop his ass. On some real shit. But they do this behind they TV screen. Tough guys. Internet tough guys. You know how many times I've been called nigga to my face?
> Mzmygrane: How many?
> Silentassassin321: None. You know how many times I've been called nigga online?
> Mzmygrane: How many?
> Silentassassin321: Too many ta' count. You know what that tells me?
> Mzmygrane: What?
> Silentassassin321: Of the dozens of white dudes I see every day, most of them I call friend, at least two ah' three wanna call me nigga.

This elaboration was extremely problematic for me to fathom and made me question even more why Microsoft had not created a better system to ward off verbal abuse resulting from linguistic profiling. This situation fueled in this gaming space seems to be creating a hostile environment for this gamer to assume that white men he encounters want to call him "nigger." Black-sounding gamers were inherently deviant because of linguistics and they were immediately punished based on how they sounded.

A second issue associated with the occurrences of hate is the speed at which the racist events occur and quickly expire. I am not sure if this was a good sign that they brushed off this act of ignorance or a bad sign—a gamer such as *silentassassin321* might harbor his feelings of being victimized, which may explain his hostility. Many males of color I encountered normalized this behavior as something that constantly occurs within Xbox Live.

> *ChrisisNice*: Man this happens all the time. It ain't nothing new. And Xbox don't care. We just expect it. Sometimes it can happen e'er day. That's what if I'm not playin' wit my boys, then I ain't even on the mic.

Many blacks have normalized negative situations in their lives—the constant presence of police, violence in inner cities, poverty, racism, etc.—and this is one instance where the normalization process occurs again. Even as I mentioned before, video games have also become a site of normalizing stereotypical black life. By normalizing these events and by not filing complaints against offending gamers, there is no way for oppressed gamers to stress this problem to Microsoft. This failure to report racist incidents only confirms Microsoft's stance that there is no problem within the space. Many of the males of color that I encountered had long given up on Microsoft to punish gamers for their racist acts within Xbox Live.

> *ChrisIsNice:* Shit we just deal wit it like we deal wit all dis otha shit in our lives. . . . hoods fucked up. We in and outta jail. Ain't no fucking jobs. And white folks gon do what they do best. Ignore the shit they created. So why should we expect anything less from dey ass on Xbox?

The third most important aspect outlined in the excerpt is that racist acts within Xbox Live are fueled merely by how a gamer sounds, linguistic profiling. First, the gaming room was filled with mostly males who sounded African-American or black Latino, and they mostly used Ebonics to speak with one another. The type of English a gamer is using is extremely important to note. Within the excerpt, I noted the gamers who were using Standard American English. I didn't want to assume that they were Caucasian but they sounded like white males, and their avatars were white and male. This mere technological advance negates what many utopians hope for within the space—no one has to know you're a dog. This may have been the case within text-based communities, but the presence of voice creates particular challenges in disguising the real-world self. As all of the males described in the interviews, their only "sin" was their "skin" and they didn't have the "complexion for the protection." Xbox just became an extension of black life in a white world and there was no place for them.

4.2 PUNISHING BLACKNESS IN POPULAR MEDIA

As was previously explained, deviance is a term that refers to behavior that does not conform to socially accepted norms. Here I focus solely on the deviant bodies that the deviant acts of racism, sexism, and other oppressions are enacted upon. The previous chapters have illustrated that women and racial minorities experience marginalization because of their virtual bodies through linguistic profiling. This chapter will explore the intersecting realities of women of color considering the amplification effect of their ascribed identities. But before going into a discussion on intersecting identities, it is first important to situate why the identity of blackness is often punished the most harshly in the space. This will need to be considered and examined before exploring the reality of black women within Xbox Live.

As Terry and Urla (1995) explain, deviant social behavior "manifests in the materiality of the body" (p. 2). However, not all bodies within Xbox Live are subject to the label of deviant. Most often, blackness and any association with blackness are punished violently within the space. As Mohanram (1999) explains, "blackness is a discursive practice exercised by the confluence of history, economics, geography, and language" (p. xiv) and these spaces continue to expand. Blackness has been constructed in a manner that enables and is enabled by its counterpart—whiteness (Mohanram, 1999). She writes: "first whiteness has the ability to move; second the ability to move results in the unmarking of the body. In contrast, blackness is signified through a marking and is always static and immobilizing" (Mohanram, 1999, p. 4). As the relativist view of deviance would confirm, this embodiment is a process rather than a given, and in order to sustain this meaning, it must constantly and continuously be articulated and performed, which is what occurs within Xbox Live— "inequitable power relationships between various spaces and places are rearticulated as the inequitable power between races" (Mohanram, 1999, p. 3). As Razack (2002) explains, "...racial hierarchies come into existence through patriarchy and capitalism, each system of domination constituting the other" (p. 6). Digital spaces (users and owners) are now reflective of this patriarchal, capitalist structure confirming the hegemonic domination of whiteness.

An area that best illustrates how blackness, particularly black masculinity, is punished most harshly is through criminal sanctions and legal outcomes. The black criminal emerged from the myth of Stagolee (Lee Shelton) in the late nineteenth century. In folklore, Stagolee was often portrayed as a hyperviolent gangster and pimp. Yet, despite his negative image, he was often glorified by disenfranchised black men who viewed him as a symbol of defiance and power. This symbol eventually became a symbol of empowerment in some communities, and the image actually began to be popularized in media (Blaxploitation films, music, news, etc.). The next section will explore four paradigms of criminalizing black masculinity that have led to this identity being punished most harshly in public and private spaces, virtual worlds included.

4.2.1 The Resistant Masculinity Paradigm

The marginalization of black men begins with their failure to attain power and the perpetual state of Three-Fifths a person. Some scholars suggest this has never been rectified (Berlin, 1998). But many black men have resisted this eternal state of inhumanity and have fought back and resisted. Resistant masculinity is the first theme that has been popularized in media and also punished most harshly in physical spaces. Resistant masculinity, as the first paradigm, refers to the fact that black men were forced to resist oppression during slavery and assert their masculinity in a society that tried to emasculate them (Wright, 2010, p. 13). Scholars define the paradigm of resistant masculinity as an attempt by black men to resist oppression and assert their masculinity in a society that sought to strip away any sense of manhood. There is a correlation between white southern manhood and slavery where white men established their masculinity by using slavery to make black men inferior to them. This is apparent in black and white men's interactions in Xbox Live. As the previous chapter illustrated, the mere presence of blackness incites many males to lash out aggressively toward black masculinity in the space. In turn, many black males within Xbox Live will reassert their manhood and masculinity and attempt to reclaim the power that is trying to be usurped and diminished in the space. This observation goes to the notion of the self-made man paradigm.

4.2.2 The Self-Made Masculinity Paradigm

Michael Kimmel (1996) discusses the paradigm of self-made masculinity discussing the standard of manhood situated in the new standard of individual achievement. Although black men were excluded from being considered self-made men, a concept mostly associated with the privileges of white masculinity, many historical black men were able to achieve despite impossible odds. For instance, Booker T. Washington was able to establish strong relationships with white philanthropists and political figures to raise money to establish the Tuskegee Institute, which was the most influential black institution in the early twentieth century (Wright, 2010). Unfortunately, popular media has deviated from positive images of self-made black men such as Adam Clayton Powell and Malcolm X to inner-city stories of black youth attempting to attain the American Dream but mostly through illegal means. Media has popularized greed, extreme materialism, and capitalism as core tenets of self-made men within Blaxploitation films and music. Given this reality, black masculinity is not only punished in private and public spaces, they are devalued for failing to attain to this norm established by whiteness and masculinity. Comments directed toward black men in Xbox Live consistently reference laziness, the lack of attaining employment, drug dealing, etc. These images have been created by not affording black men the ability to become self-made men or by punishing them when in fact they do become self-made men.

4.2.3 The Black Rage Paradigm

Black rage and violence are prevalent in the retelling of Stagolee and is very popular within media. As Rosevelt Noble Jr suggests, black rage is defined as "a response to black suffering and failure, which is exacerbated by irresistible temptation to attribute African-American problems to a history of white racist oppression" (as cited in Wright, 2010, p. 25). It can also be viewed as a reaction to the black man's frustration with his lack of power and inability to exercise his manhood without being punished. The expression of rage has constantly worked against the black man.

Historically and in contemporary media, black men have been portrayed as innately violent beasts. The rage that was perceived to have been carried out on white men soon transitioned into rage carried out on white women. The myth of the black man as a violent sexual predator began to characterize black masculinity, especially in news and other popular media outlets, and this in turn led to extreme punishment and penalty, most notably lynching, as the excerpt from Wright illustrates below:

> Historian Winthrop Jordan argues that the White man's objection of the black man's sexuality was essentially a projection of his own fears and desires. It was the White man who committed sexual aggression against the blacks. By transferring the blame to the Negro's "libidinous nature," the White man made the black man bear his burden of sexual guilt, according to Jordan. This myth of the black man's penis and strong libido was used to excuse the murder of thousands of southern black men at the hands of White lynch mobs (as cited in Wright, 2010, p. 26).

4.2.4 The Plantation Patriarchy Paradigm

Plantation patriarchy refers to the model of manhood demonstrated by white men on southern plantations during slavery (Wright, 2010). As bell hooks reveals, plantation patriarchy is situated in white supremacy and white men's need to dominate anyone that they consider inferior. Hooks also dubs this paradigm as patriarchal masculinity. This stemmed from the need of white men to justify slavery. She also rightly points out that black men soon adopted this same approach in dealing with their wives and families, realizing that plantation patriarchy is inherently unequal along gender lines. This led to divides among black men and women upon emancipation. Because of black men's lack of power, they began to utilize the few privileges afforded to them as men, male privilege. This is demonstrated in the ways that black men communicate with women in Xbox Live. Sexism is very prevalent and black women constantly suggested that black men were just as oppressive to them as white men were to them. The example below highlights this reality:

> *cdXFemmeFataleXcd:* When I started gaming, of course, like all of us, we played with guys. At first, the dudes liked that we were a part of their groups and we would hang out with them all the time. You remember that right?
> *Mzmygrane:* Oh yeah. Wake-n-game right? We couldn't wait to get online.
> *cdXFemmeFataleXcd:* Well they started getting too comfortable and I guess they true colors started coming through. They started calling us bitches. Started saying all kind of nasty shit. Suck my dick this suck my dick that. But we were like tokens. Especially for those of us who were good. They paraded us around like trophies. We were supposed to be seen and not heard.
> *Mzmygrane:* Oh yeah. Mascots.
> *cdXFemmeFataleXcd:* Exactly.

I contend that black men act in this sexist to exert their power and privilege of masculinity. They are not afforded the full privileges of masculinity within the space and could be viewed as still Three-Fifths a person within the space. Some black men, in acting out their masculine privilege over time, have adopted white masculine ideology in their dealings with women, and Xbox is not exempt from these racialized and gendered relationships.

4.3 INTERSECTING IDENTITIES AND INTERSECTING OPPRESSIONS

Not to negate the seriousness of anyone's experiences in Xbox Live, but I contend that women of color experience undue amounts of oppression due to the intersecting nature of their identities. And their experiences are not monolithic. Although all a part of the black diaspora, the experiences of African-American and Latina women vary to some degree.

4.3.1 Black Women and Intersectionality

Intersectionality, although conceptualized through black women's experiences, can be explicated to incorporate any marginalized identity. As its base, intersectionality recognizes that we each can embody privilege and subordination, but that subordinate status is influenced by the amplification of the many layers associated with our oppressed identities. Black feminists write extensively about the tactics and strategies of black women to resist sexism and racism. Lorde (1981), through her experiences in the second wave, rearticulated the amplification of oppressions due to intersecting identities. She comments that "there's always someone asking you to underline one piece of yourself—whether it's black, woman, mother, dyke, teacher, etc—because that's the piece they need to key in to ... to dismiss everything else" (p. 717). Her statement exemplifies our desire to make sense of the social world by categorizing others to gain information with little effort. But this process leads to the ignoring of multiple social categories in which we all embody. By employing an intersectional approach in which to view not only women of color but also other marginalized communities, we gain a better understanding of the interaction between one's many social identities and the influences of different social structures on the construction of these identities (Stewart & McDermott, 2004).

Crenshaw (1991) employed an intersectional approach in her examination of the legal consequences of violence against women of color in the United States. She employed the term to explain the ways that race and gender, among other ascribed identities, "interact to shape the multiple dimensions of black women's . . . experiences" (p. 1244). Further, in trying to understand the experiences of black women, it is only possible to look at the dualism of racism and sexism, as trying to separate these experiences fails to capture the full dimensions of these experiences. Additionally, Collins (1998) stresses the dangers of examining identifiers such as gender, race, and class as "distinctive social hierarchies" (p. 63), but rather looking intersectionally to see how each identifier informs and constructs the other. As it relates to the women I interviewed for this project, they embody multiple identities and have experienced discriminatory acts based on these ascribed identifiers. To combat these oppressive structures within Xbox Live, many women and people of color have created their own gaming spaces to resist these hegemonic structures of dominance.

Intersectionality recognizes the specificity and multiplicity of differently located women's social locations. Crenshaw (1989) first articulated this theory to address the complicated and compounding nature of oppression. The work of Collins (2000) also focuses on the experiences of marginalized women. Her work helps to contextualize specific oppressions within the macro context of systemic oppression based on gender, race, class, sexual orientation, ability, and additional social locations, which are central to this research. She theorizes a concept called the matrix of domination, which is a way to map oppressions that can be used to show social organization within which intersecting oppressions originate, develop, and are contained (p. 227). This matrix demonstrates how oppression is socially organized and traces how knowledge construction influences empowerment. It also illustrates the social organization and institutionalization of oppression. Collins also points out that the matrix of domination will vary from context to context and is historically specific, while also showing "how domination and oppression is structured across time, within any context" (p. 228).

4.3.2 Latina and Chicana Identity Development and Oppression

A Chicana identity encompasses challenges that are distinct from white women and other women of color (Vera & De los Santos, 2005). Chicana feminists' realities encompass multiple identities that include ethnicity, gender, and acculturation issues. Pesquera and Segura (1997) describe the Chicana's experience as including a "triple lens of oppression" where she must deal with issues related to gender, race, ethnicity, class, and the interaction of these within her culture of origin and the dominant culture in which she lives. That is, Chicanas must learn to balance multiple identities where they struggle to maintain their cultural identity while acculturating to the dominant culture. In her book entitled *Borderlands: La Frontera*, Anzaldúa (1987) explains that women of Mexican descent must straddle two cultures that border each other. She states that a merging of these two worlds creates a new identity, *la mestiza*, who is skilled at being flexible and copes by tolerating cultural inconsistencies. Women of Mexican descent often experience pressure to uphold the expectations from both her ethnic group and the dominant culture. Anzaldúa (1987) asserts that this dilemma illustrates the *neplanta* stage where one becomes aware of constantly shifting or adapting to different cultural expectations and language. From this struggle, *la mestiza* develops a political consciousness that focuses on the elimination of the racial, ethnic, and gender oppression she experiences. Despite work to understand the Chicana identity formation, scarce literature exists on understanding how Chicanas negotiate identities. Even less scholarship has been devoted to Puerto Rican women, but their experiences are very similar to the experiences of Chicanas.

Traditional identity theories do not include the complexity of Latina identity. The concept of identity is complex since it can include membership in several groups that are associated with various statuses. Several identity theories limit their focus on understanding the internal coherence of identity or an overall identity (Marcia, 1966). Conversely, other theories examine social identities separately, failing to include the possibility of intersections of these identities. For example, studies examining specific identities, such as ethnicity, ignore the role of gender in defining his or her ethnic identity (Deux & Stewart, 2001). Similarly, looking solely at gender as a variable excludes contextual factors, such as culture, that influence gender identity. Examining gender and ethnicity separately ignores how socialization and societal ideology affect the self (Dukes & Martinez, 1994; Martinez & Dukes, 1991).

The excerpt below examines the Latina experience within Xbox Live, recognizing the complexities of Latinas' intersecting identities:

XpkX RicanMami: All I know is that only people just like you understand you. So there's no way you can understand where we coming from. Now I know you being African-American and all you understand some of the struggle. But since we Latina as well, we got added shit to deal with. Again, not to take away nothin' from you as a Black woman. Ok? So don't get mad, I'm just being real like you want me to right?

Mzmygrane: Yes that's all I want . . .

XpkX RicanMami: Ok ok ok . . . But the point I was makin' first is that people look at me and assume I'm not American. They think I'm a fucking illegal just cuz I'm Hispanic. So I got the race thing, the gender thing, and the citizenship thing to deal wit.

Mzmygrane: I feel you. Language too.

XpkX RicanMami: Shit yeah you right. Just cuz I talk with an accent people think I can't speak English good. I just wish more Blacks would understand where we comin' from. We ain't trying to take over as the most oppressed. Ain't no damn contest who the most fucked up minority is in this country. We all fucked up. I just wish people would recognize that we got it hard too. Especially Black people.

Mzmygrane: Well answer this question for me. Why do you identify as Black since you seem to be separating yourself from them? Well us? Umm Blacks?

XpkX RicanMami: Cuz I consider myself Black. As my race. Ain't no brown category to mark. Ethnically, I am Latino or Hispanic or whatever. Now it is fucked up that I get to choose what race I identify the most with. Even though it ain't no way to measure it, I would never consider choosing White cuz I don't identify with the privilege of whiteness. Now I got a lot of family that choose White and they say it makes life easier. I just feel that's selling out.

Mzmygrane: Oh oh a sell out huh. Like you called me before?

XpkX RicanMami: (*Laughing*) Nah ma. I was just trippin' out at first. Cuz you sound mad White for real. Then you come into the room talking all Angela Davis and shit, I was like who the fuck is this! But you cool ma. Fa real.

Mzmygrane: Oh yeah. I'm good. I got four of y'all so that's straight. But back to what you said. Why you think your family is selling out by saying White?

XpkX RicanMami: I just think that people of color need to stick together. We all oppressed. We all a part of the same struggle.

The combination of statuses one holds in society can create a multitude of discriminations and challenges. It is possible that structured inequalities reinforce each other (Jefferies & Ransford, 1980; Martinez & Dukes, 1991). It is difficult to distinguish which part of their identity society is targeting when Latinas encounter systemic obstacles or negative life experiences. This uncertainty can lead many Latinas to define themselves situationally and focus on understanding how to attend to the expectations of others (Ferdman & Gallegos, 2001). Martinez and Dukes (1991) argue that being a minority woman creates multiple disadvantages created by ethnicity and gender, which they termed ethgender. They assert that the combination of being a woman, being a member of an ethnic minority group, and the interaction of cultural roles in the dominant and one's ethnic group is a triple disadvantage.

Razack and Fellows (1998) define interlocking oppression as the ways in which systems of oppression come into existence in and through one another. By this logic, class exploitation cannot be accomplished without gender and racial hierarchies, or imperialism could not function without class exploitation, sexism, or heterosexism. Interlocking oppression accounts for how awareness of race, class, gender (as well as other social locations) co-constitute one another in ways that cannot be separated in white supremacist capitalist patriarchy (Razack & Fellows, 1998, p. 3). Interlocking oppression conceptualizes the intricacy of social locations in relation to one another and the process of how one's identity is constructed against those of others. Intersectionality elaborates on the way the social locations of individuals have multiple axes, which form their complex subjectivities. Intersectionality understands that aspects of identity do not function independently. As the next chapter will illustrate, because of the intersecting oppressions experienced, women have resisted these oppressions and deviant acts by using resources within the space to their own advantage.

PART *III*

The Solutions

CHAPTER 5

Deviant Bodies Resisting Deviant Acts

XpkX MammaMia: I don't know why you getting so crunk, we just [f*expletive] around. Ain't nothing impressive by this [s*expletive].

Mzmygrane: But yeah it is. You guys are doing something to fight back. It's very impressive. Give me some examples of what you actually do and then tell me why you do it?

XpkX MammaMia: Aight, umm, well we started off just player killing. Especially in games where it was friendly fire. Now we used to just grief out on dudes that would [f*expletive] wit us. You know saying all that [we're] illegal [s*expletive], go back to Mexico crap. But then we just said [f*expletive] it, let's grief out on all of 'em.

Mzmygrane: Now when you say grief, what do you actually mean?

XpkX MammaMia: Well I know a lot of folks grief just to be dicks. But we doing it for a purpose. We have a reason. But we really just want to keep guys from enjoying the game. They keep us from enjoying the game by not welcoming women fully so this is the only way we can repay them. It's not like Xbox gives a [f*expletive]. And funny thing. You know *Blaze* actually got suspended for griefing. She got so many complaints they suspended her account. And all the complaints we [f*expletive] filed for racism and sexism [s*expletive] and nothing happened. But then we decide to do something, finally stick it to the man *(laughing)* and we get punished. I like how you define us, as deviants. That's so true. We get punished all the time.

(Gray, 2011, pp. 161—162)

The above excerpt is an actual interview conducted with a woman of color organizing in Xbox Live with others like her. In her interview, she actually describes that she is fed up with dealing with the racism, sexism, heterosexism, and nativism by the default gamer in Xbox Live. This chapter highlights their experiences, among others, and situates them within the literature or digital activism or collective organizing and Information Communication Technologies (ICTs). It is imperative to examine if their efforts can be sustained to elicit actual change within the space.

5.1 INFORMATION COMMUNICATION TECHNOLOGY AND WOMEN ORGANIZING ONLINE

We are steadily witnessing the appropriation of new communication technologies to facilitate collective organizing and mobilization. As

Eltantawy and Wiest (2011) explain, the development of social media creates opportunities for digital- and web-based social movements to change the reality of collective action. Cyberactivists have incorporated a host of tools to facilitate their organization activities, from staging boycotts, to staging public protests and planning demonstrations, among others (Langman, 2005). The types of new communication technologies that have been used include short messaging services (SMS), social networking sites, and as this book highlights, virtual gaming communities. Typically, one would not assume that collective organizing and resistance would take place inside a virtual gaming community. But this is exactly where a cohort of female gamers of color experience and resist hegemonic inequality every day. This chapter will explore methods utilized for their online activism associated with their struggles with racism, sexism, heterosexism, and other intersecting oppressions. They have responded with various in-game tactics to counter the perceived source of their (linguistic) oppression, the default gamer. By situating their methods within the larger context of third-wave feminism, social movements, and online resistance, I examine if these tactics are reminiscent of actual collective organizing, merely reflect individual acts of resistance, or are simply griefing activities used to disrupt gameplay and harass other players.

Extensive research has been conducted on web activism and how information communication technologies can be used as a tool to facilitate participation within social movements (Crow & Longford, 2004; Friesen, 2004; Garrett, 2006). The literature describes three mechanisms that potentially link ICTs and participation although each can be debated: reduction of participation costs, promotion of collective identity, and creation of community. Leizerov (2000) explains how ICTs help to reduce costs associated with publishing and accessing information. This helps with the flow of information, which in turn can increase participation. The Internet enables communication between many individuals instead of information stemming from one central location. With the aid of Internet technologies, people can follow a variety of links to acquire a full range of different and competing perspectives on almost any issue, with or without the politics, financial limitations, and the nature of coverage provided by other mass media (Poor, 2005). By surfing the Internet, people can easily explore alternative new sources and perspectives on their own time without having to accept only the most publicized messages through print, radio, and television.

Bonchek (1995) claims that ICTs help to lower communication and coordination costs, which facilitates group formation, recruitment, retention, and efficiency. This example is best illustrated through black women's organizing with the Million Woman's March. The preparation involved with the Million Woman's March was one of the earliest attempts by women to empower themselves using digital technologies. Even though women used the Internet and other digital technologies regularly, this early attempt was the result of media not supporting black women to publicize their event. The event was organized around the idea of reinventing black families and communities. Further, they articulated for the continuation of black political and economic justice and fundamental social change.

Everett (2009) writes extensively about not focusing on what hinders women's progress in technology, but rather on what women have already accomplished within technology and what needs to be done to ensure more can take part. Major media outlets had previously positioned black women outside of digital technologies, often citing the disproportionate rate of computer technology diffusion within the black community and rarely mentioning how many within the black community had found ingenious ways to utilize Internet technologies.

Black women certainly aided in the diminishing of the "digital divide" leading up to October 25, 1997, in the organizing and planning of the Million Woman March on Philadelphia. During the preparation stages, mainstream media was not at all interested in advertising or supporting this event. Further, when the event transpired, there were only brief snippets of coverage provided by CNN or C-SPAN. Media critics began questioning the lack of media motivation—revealing to the world what was obvious to the black community. *The Los Angeles Sentinel* just 2 years earlier in discussing media coverage of the Million Man March questioned if the coverage of the event would have been more extensive and comprehensive if it had erupted in violence. Orderly black bodies interrupt the traditional frames created by mainstream media outlets—riots, criminal acts, poor, etc. The media was accustomed to stereotypical images of black women which are all controlled by dominant ideology. But the media's lack of support for this event challenged a prevailing notion of blacks, specifically black women, regarding information technologies—computer literacy and the digital divide. Black women were often flaunted as poster children for the digital divide, highlighting their lack of access to computers and lack of knowledge of the Internet. Television and print media had been long sources for white communities in organizing while the black community relied on ground and local efforts to mobilize.

Despite the lack of advertising and support by major media outlets, these black women were able to successfully organize by employing the Internet to coordinate their efforts. These "low-tech, low-profile, urban women had compelled the racially biased mainstream media to cover in fact (the event's success) what they ignored in theory (its very possibility)" (Everett, 2009, p. 52). These women were able to accomplish this feat by merging new and old technologies to ensure inclusivity of unwired women. These black women moved beyond "technology consumers and laborers" into "technology innovators and producers" (p. 58). What began as an online effort soon moved to the streets and ultimately to the mainstream media. Reflecting back on the mechanisms that link ICTs and participation, the women in this example highlight how a reduction of participation costs with the promotion of a collective identity lead to the creation and mobilization of their organized community.

The second mechanism linking ICTs and participation in social movements, the promotion of a collective identity, is important to discuss women organizing in Xbox Live. Studies demonstrate how ICTs may be able to foster collective identity across a dispersed population which organizers can then mobilize in support of collective action (Brainard & Siplon, 2000; Myers, 2000). Rogers and Singhal (2003) describe efforts to organize individuals lacking power within a community into groups where they can be empowered through communicating with others similar to themselves. Empowerment allows people to have a say in the outcome of their existence, and communication via ICTs is a mechanism through which empowerment may be accomplished. Taylor and Whittier (1992) identify three elements of collective identity in social movements: (1) individuals share a sense of solidarity when they define shared characteristics as being relevant and important; (2) individuals harbor a consciousness, which is a shared interpretative framework that includes political consciousness, relational networks, and the environment of action of the movement; and (3) when there is a culture of direct opposition to the dominant order. Xbox Live and the default gamer exist as the dominant order. Women and people of color, by failing to conform to the norm of the white male, are in direct opposition to what was intended. Xbox Live, as being a part of the gaming culture, is not exempt from criticism in sustaining a culture of masculinity and whiteness. There are numerous examples of activism that has been diminished and this chapter will soon highlight those stories.

The third mechanism identified linking ICTs and participation in social movements is the creation of community (Garrett, 2006). Scholars have written extensively on the role of ICTs on an individual's sense of community (Haythornthwaite & Wellman, 2004; Wellman, 2002; Wellman et al., 2001). Scholars suggest that information communication technologies are facilitating the maintenance of geographically dispersed face-to-face networks (Brainard & Siplon, 2000). The Internet provides the means to move away from communities based on physical locations and traditions toward communities based on collective interests and identities wherever they may be located in the world, providing they have Internet connectivity. Additionally, Uhler Cart (1997) argues that ICTs can possibly serve as a means of support for community among groups that experience prejudice and domination. The women within Xbox Live illustrate how ICTs serve as a medium through which identity support is provided and facilitated through virtual forums, chat, and organized efforts within the game.

5.2 EXAMINING THE ORGANIZED EFFORTS OF WOMEN IN XBOX LIVE

Scholars who examine activism recognize that it should be defined along a continuum. This continuum represents a range of activities, including clicking one's support on a web site, volunteering, organization involvment, etc. The women's behaviors examined in the previous chapter can also be viewed along a continuum—from the individualistic approach to the collective. But it is important to not only privilege the experiences of these women within Xbox Live but to also situate their efforts within the literature to evaluate the utility of their organizing. Within academic literature, digital activism falls into three general areas. Vegh (2003) classifies these as Awareness/Advocacy, Organization/Mobilization, and Action/Reaction.

1. Awareness/Advocacy—the primary uses of the Internet in online advocacy revolve around organizing the movement and carrying

out an action. The process for online advocacy can focus on organizing and mobilizing a group of people for action, or actually carrying out an effort with a particular goal in mind.

2. Organization/Mobilization—is the decision to proceed with an action in online or offline contexts. The Internet is used for mobilization in three different ways: (1) to coordinate online action (such as e-mail with logistics of place and time to meet), (2) for a call to action that normally happens offline, but can more efficiently be done online, or (3) for an online action that can only be carried out online.

3. Action/Reaction—online activism is comprised of proactive actions to achieve a certain goal or of reactive actions against controls and authorities imposing them.

The actions of the women discussed here fall within each of the three categories, which will be explained using an actual in-game resistive stragety to illustrate.

> *Mzmygrane*: Ok so I know why you do it, I want some examples of what you do. Are there certain types of games where you do certain things? Walk me through some examples.
>
> *Patroa917*: Oh yeah. You see the most in Modern Warfare since Gears doesn't have friendly fire on. Let's just play a round so you can see firsthand.
> *(Several minutes pass while we both prepare to play a match)*
> *Patroa917*: Ok everything depends on the map. So if we get Wetwork, or Bog, or Ambush *(names of maps from Call of Duty 4: Modern Warfare)*, we just hang out in the back and spawn kill.
> *(Waiting for game to load)*
> *Patroa917*: Aight bet. We got Bog. Now you go to the otha side and hang out behind that crate. Or just hang wherever our teammates are and kill em.
> *(We are in a game mode called Hardcore where friendly fire is enabled meaning we can kill our teammates)*
> *Mzmygrane:* Umm. Kill our teammates? What about the other team?
> *Patroa917*: Kill em all. Shit! Spawn kill them and friendly kill us! Well not me *(laughing)*.
> *Mzmygrane*: Ok. Umm. What purpose does this serve?
> *Patroa917*: No purpose. Just making everybody mad. We can make our team mad of course by killin em. And we make the opposing team mad by spawn killing. Everybody pissed off and it makes me happy.
> *Mzmygrane*: How often do you do this? Every day? Every time you play?
> *Patroa917*: Nah. Most of the time it's not just random like we doin now. We mostly do it after somebody piss us off. Oh shit. You see that shit *(she sniped someone's head off)*.
> *(We complete several games and engage in the same behavior. By this time, I have several messages of gamers complaining about my actions. Several*

gamers also submitted complaints on my actions within the game. I continue resistance griefing with Patroa917 and ignore the messages. Our game plan changes when we play a map called Ambush.)
Patroa917: Oh shit let's have suhmo' fun. Follow me. *(I follow her towards the middle of map near the fence)*
Patroa917: Ok pull out the pistol and jump up and down on my head.
Mzmygrane: Ok what's supposed to happen?
Patroa917: Just wait for it. See what I'm doing is looking down . . .
Mzmygrane: Oh shit hell naw. Now what do I do?
(I have glitched outside of the map which is another griefing tactic—stretching the limits of the architecture of the map to your advantage.)
Patroa917: Kill anybody you see. Well except me. They won't know where the hell it's coming from. Not unless they see you. Oh kill yourself when you run outta bullets.
Mzmygrane: (Laughing) Hell naw. Ok.
(I successfully kill my teammates and the opposing team. When I run out of bullets, I kill myself and begin the process over again. By this point, I have about a dozen messages of players complaining about my behavior within the space.)
Patroa917: Oh good shit. Blaze n Boss are online. We got fo' (four) folks so let's get on Gears. Put yo gears in mygrane. We'll start off wit some of dat griefing shit as you call it.

(Gray, 2011, 173–174)

The above excerpt illustrates one of the tactics employed by women of color in Xbox Live to combat the oppression they experience on a daily basis. This excerpt reveals that women will reappropriate resources within the game for their own means. So as Awareness/Advocacy highlights, Internet technologies in any medium can be used to carry out an action and organize. Many female clans within Xbox Live have illustrated the importance of using digital tools to aid in resisting oppressions. As another all-female clan demonstrated, their efforts to resist are sometimes advertised in Xbox Live forums attempting to gain a critical mass of women to engage in these behaviors. So the actual Xbox Live infrastructure has been employed to deliver messages to one another to coordinate their resistance campaigns, and many often use Xbox Live forums to advertise their efforts before and after it occurs. Unfortunately, many of these forums are deleted by the Microsoft administrator for violating Terms of Service. According to many gamers, this happens often. But ironically, inflammatory comments that openly use racist, sexist, and otherwise offensive speech remain on the message boards and are never taken down, even when flagged.

The above excerpt also illustrates that Organization/Mobilization is an extremely important tenet of digital activism but is not always employed by the marginalized groups. One clan in particular, the *Concscious Daughters* in Xbox Live, not only wanted to mobilize women within Xbox Live, but they actually sought to connect and foster a sense of community in physical spaces as well. They wanted to continue their actions in an offline context. The excerpt below illustrates their desire:

> *MissUnique*: I get so tired of not being able to do shit about it [racism, sexism]. I mean we helpless and filing complaints won't work.
> *Mzmygrane:* Do you think there are actual solutions to the problem?
> *MissUnique*: Yeah but we can't do it ourselves. We need all gamers who care about this shit to do something.
> *Mzmygrane:* So you mean like marching on Microsoft?
> *(laughing)*
> *MissUnique*: Shit. Hell yeah! Nah but on some real shit at least do something so they know that it's a real problem. And so that other women know that they not by they'selves.
> *Mzmygrane:* What kinds of things have you done outside of Xbox that might help?
> *MissUnique*: Other than boycotting—which nobody did. Other than making forums that get taken down. I don't know what to do. I'll keep blogging about it and keep getting hated on and keep getting called bitch. Other than that. I don't know what to do.

MissUnique expressed extreme disappointment in not being able to effect meaningful change in Xbox Live. But without the ability to generate widespread support among women in Xbox as well as male gamers, she suggests her efforts are in vain. But her efforts illustrate an important tenet of digital activism.

These examples also highlight *Action/Reaction*, which is the third tenet of digital activism. To reiterate, it focuses on proactive actions to achieve a certain goal. It also focuses on reactive actions against the authority imposing them. The fact that women in Xbox Live constantly file complaints and post forums in the Xbox.com site highlights a continued engagement in hoping things change in Xbox Live. But from the interviews conducted, it seems that their actions fall just short of the intended goal. The structure of the space seems to ensure this. The forums are created and are immediately removed by the Xbox.com administrator for violating Terms of Service. So even if they wanted to engage and resist the authority of Xbox Live, it is impossible to do so. But they consistently reappropriate the tools within the space to attempt to resist domination within the space. This process can be examined through the lens of resource mobilization theory.

5.2.1 Resource Mobilization Theory

Resource mobilization theory emerged during the 1970s as a reaction to collective behavior models that attempted to explain how people with little power were able to organize, resist, and/or challenge those in power (Oberschall, 1973, p. 102). Resource mobilization theories suggest that participants within a movement are rational actors and decision-makers (Calhoun, 1993), and collective behavior should be understood in terms of the logic and costs and benefits as well as opportunities for action (Larana et al., 1994, p. 5). An important assumption within resource mobilization theory is that groups engaged in social movements should have the opportunity to challenge those in power (Jenkins, 1983). Extending this premise further, McCarthy and Zald (1977) recognize that the resource mobilization approach emphasizes both support and constraint of societal forces (what can hurt can also help). It also examines the multitude of resources that could be utilized to support the movement as well as other groups that can aid and assist. Resource mobilization theory also recognizes that movements are dependent upon external support for success. With these factors in mind, resource mobilization theory can aid in the understanding of how social movements emerge and develop and become successful (Melucci, 1989; Meyer & Tarrow, 1998).

Important to women and people of color in Xbox Live, it is important to gauge the literature on virtual organizing and understand the dynamics for a virtual community to be successful in their social change. To reach this point, it is important to know that there are two main perspectives within resource mobilization: (1) the organizational—entrepreneurial perspective (McCarthy & Zald, 1977); and (2) the political process perspective (Gamson, 1975; McAdam, 1982). As Gamson (1975) argues, an organization is required for a group to launch a social protest or movement. Early resource mobilization theory considers that strong, bureaucratically structured social organizing is crucial for a successful movement (McCarthy & Zald, 1977). On the other hand, the current research does not have that type of organization structured as described by McCarthy and Zald (1977). The current research reflects a virtual organization, and as Ahuja and Carley (1998) describe, a virtual organization is an organization that's geographically distributed and bound by a long-term common interest or goal. Most importantly, a virtual organization communicates and coordinates through information technology.

By employing ICTs, members of virtual teams are able to communicate electronically from different geographic locations and are able to virtually organize. Several key characteristics of a virtual organization have been identified by scholars. First, a virtual organization is not bound by borders (Kristof, Brown, Sims, & Smith, 1995; Mowshowitz, 1997; Travica, 2005) and exists for a specific goal (Ahuja & Carley, 1998; Foster, Kesselman, & Tuecke, 2001). Within this borderless, virtual system, membership and organizational structure change over time (Travica, 2005). In addition, a virtual organization relies on an electronic network (Grenier & Metes, 1995; Lipnack & Stamps, 1997; Travica, 2005) and uses advanced information technology to facilitate the movement. Given that, a virtual organization is assumed to be able to quickly unify a group, even though the resources, services, and people that comprise a virtual organization can be single- or multi-institutional, homogenous, or heterogeneous (Travica, 2005).

Resource mobilization theorists posit that after a group or a movement has organized to some extent, there are certain factors which will influence its success. Cohen (1985) argues that success is enhanced by the ability to mobilize resources, gain recognition from those in power, and have flexible organization, among other things. Linking to groups in power has a direct impact on a group's ability to launch a successful movement. The more supportive connections the social movement has with groups in power, the greater the likelihood of the group's success (Aveni, 1978; McCarthy & Zald, 1977). However, being linked to a powerful group is not always possible among groups organized for change. Another factor which may influence the success of a social movement is the choice of strategies and tactics. Jenkins (1983) reviews resource mobilization theory and classifies three types of tactics used with elites: (1) persuasion, (2) bargaining, and (3) coercion. Another factor which needs to be taken into consideration in evaluating a social movement is the structure of the group itself. Jenkins (1983) argues that groups which are organized bureaucratically are effective in fighting technical battles but not effective in mobilizing grassroots support. Given the virtual nature of the current research, tactics and strategies have to be adapted to fit the space. Also, measuring success must be modified to fit the overall goal of those organizing.

5.2.2 Applying Habitus to Marginalized Gamers in Xbox

It is important to briefly examine the theoretical framework of habitus. As Holt (2008) argues, habitus emerges through beyond-conscious acts rather than strategic, rational agency. Individuals implicate themselves in their own subjection and much of this resides in the positionality of our ascribed identities. In examining the static position of one's status in a given environment, Bourdieu (1984), being both positively and negatively influenced by French structuralists, moved beyond the dualist approach of the structuralists and did not ascribe complete power to either the social structure or the individual (Calhoun, 1993; Wacquant, 1998). The deterministic approach to his work suggests that people in a society are where they are and will remain where they are because of attitudes and values they absorb as members of a particular social stratum. Most individuals are bound by their social status, whether it's low or high, and adopt the codes and symbols associated with that social position. The problem within Xbox Live is that by the nature of the space, all individuals are essentially equal—members of the same social stratum. However, because our virtual bodies bring physical world manifestations into virtuality—gender, race, class, sexuality, religion, education, etc.—we begin to replicate real-world inequalities into virtual space. So digital technologies are beginning to resemble real-world spaces, making it easier for offline inequalities to manifest online as Nakamura (2002) suggests. So even though a user may be able to leave the body behind when entering cyberspace, the real body still lingers—creating a racialized or gendered cybertype, and our "fluid selves are no less subject to cultural hegemonies, rules of conduct and regulating cultural norms than are solid ones" (Nakamura, 2002, p. 325). Kolko (2000) reinforces Nakamura's argument where she suggests that there is an inherent desire to ignore race and ethnicity in virtual worlds. She notes that the default ethnicity in most virtual communities is set to white, creating a default to whiteness for virtual worlds, replicating real-world spaces where unmarked whiteness is the cultural norm. This recreates racialized hierarchical structures present in the real world, leading to the domination of marginalized populations. This is a key component of Bourdieu's framework—the assumption that real-world privileges operate in the virtual. Members of privileged classes automatically assume these roles as they are written into social positions in which we occupy—habitus. Habitus is often referred to in Bourdieu's (1984) writings as "durable, transposable dispositions" and refers in part to the manner in which a person is raised (p. 171). All of our ways of being and ways of perceiving and approaching other individuals constitute habitus. We are not only informed by our habitus, but we in turn inform it. It is a dialectic that operates on a continuous cycle constantly reinforcing itself. For example, whiteness and masculinity are constantly reinforced in society, in schools, in government institutions, in the workplace, in TV, news, movies, and other media. It is now being reinforced in virtual communities. As Bourdieu (1984) describes, it is a "structured and structuring structure" (p. 171). Habitus is the constant programming of thinking, feeling, and acting in a particular manner, and it becomes habit forming, embodying the individual (Reay, 2004). This translates into the aggregate defining each class position and leading to the sharing of certain commonalities or codes. The larger sense of identity is captured in a group habitus containing an enduring sense and expression of who its members are, who they are not, and what relationships are between themselves and other groups. This in turn creates an invisible script that others within the group, class, or stratum learn to follow.

In the physical world, marginalized communities have a variety of responses to the inequalities they face, which, since the earliest suffrage movements, some members within groups learn to resist. Some ignore it, some aggressively oppose it, and some protest it. This scripted response is similar to the responses by marginalized populations in Xbox Live. Many members have simply normalized the inequalities they experience at the risk of appearing too sensitive or being accused of pulling the race card (Gray, 2011). Still others opt for a more aggressive approach and engage in equally offensive behavior (Gray, 2011). And others choose to organize and resist dominate structures.

5.3 CONCLUSION

Methods employed by women organizing online are largely influenced by the technology and virtual infrastructure. For instance, in the early days of the Internet, organizing was situated within e-mail list serves, discussion boards, and other multiuser domains (MUDs). These methods have evolved into web sites, blog sites, and social networking sites. And, as the examples in this book reveal, virtual gaming communities. The resistance strategies are often situated within time and space as this chapter illustrated. Women organizing and resisting in the 1960s often engaged in confrontational strategies. Organization strategies were more commonplace in the 1970s. And more electoral strategies were implemented in the 1980s. Of course, all of these methods were situated within physical spaces, and virtual space requires innovative approaches to resist and effect change. As the women in this chapter illustrated, they are using the tools that already exist in the space to offset their marginalization. They are reappropriating tools to aid in their methods of resistance. Although these methods have yet to yield any meaningful changes, their efforts highlight and engagement in resistance and mobilization.

CHAPTER 6

Virtual Tools in the Virtual House?

Highlighting Audre Lorde's speech where she famously said, "For the master's tools will never dismantle the master's house," this chapter argues for the reformation of the master's tools and cites the strategies employed by women of color within this community that speak to this radical re-envisioning. I argue that there is not one coherent movement actively mobilizing within Xbox Live but a collective of individual movements. This concluding chapter will connect their experiences and privilege all of the tactics employed by the marginalized gamers in Xbox Live. This approach is directly applicable to understanding the experiences and realities of women of color within this online gaming community—from their standpoint. Because video gaming has been constructed as an adolescent, white, male activity, the experiences of women and people of color are often overlooked. As Collins (2000, p. 185) explains, being a member of an oppressed group places one in a position to see the world differently. However, the lack of control over the apparatuses of society that sustain ideological hegemony makes the articulation of self-definition difficult.

6.1 BLACK FEMINIST THOUGHT IN THE DIGITAL ERA

> While an oppressed group's experiences may put them in a position to see things differently, their lack of control over the apparatuses of society that sustain ideological hegemony makes the articulation of their self-defined standpoint difficult.
>
> (Collins, 2000, p. 185)

Feminist scholarship continues its focus on black women's identity, still tackling controlling images by dominant groups. In 1986, Patricia Hill Collins outlined Feminist Standpoint Theory describing the unique perspective of African-American women. Ula Taylor (1998) provides an in-depth account of the four tenets of this theory: (1) self-definition and self-evaluation, (2) the interlocking nature of oppression, (3) embracing intellectual thought and political activism, and (4) the importance of culture. The above quote reflects a core tenet of black feminist theory in that creating and controlling definitions of oneself is imperative for empowerment. The oppressed have a unique standpoint in that they as individuals share particular social locations, such as gender, race, and/ or class. Further, these individuals share their meaningful experiences with one another, generating knowledge about the social world from their points of view. Despite this knowledge generation, oppressed populations lack the control needed to reframe and reconceptualize their realities. However, a particular advantage presents itself with the diffusion of information technologies, providing particular advantages to women and people of color. One of the advantages is the ability to create and control virtual spaces largely unregulated and unmolested. These spaces have the potential to foster the development of a group standpoint, negating the impact of dominant ideology.

Because of the discrimination and exclusion that many women and people of color face, they have created their own spaces within virtual worlds. Given the relative ease in which spaces can be created, this presents oppressed groups the ability of being able to control and create positive content influencing our own images (granted they are fortunate and privileged enough to have access to technology and have the skills necessary to create). For black women, the Internet provides the potential spaces in which negative representations can be thwarted disseminated through the media—mammy, jezebel, matriarch, welfare queen, bitch, ho, etc. Collins further explains that the purpose of these images is to make intersecting inequalities appear to be natural, normal, and inevitable parts of everyday life, so it is imperative for women to regain control and define our own image. But are virtual spaces that claim to be creating these alternatives reflective of this goal? Do those who are privileged enough to be able to create these virtual spaces uphold liberatory potentials or merely perpetuate stereotypes and inequalities?

The quote that opened this section was only partially completed. Before proceeding, following up on the above statement if necessary. It directly hints toward the feasibility of women actually succeeding at controlling and maintaining their own spaces: *"groups unequal in power are correspondingly unequal in their access to the resources necessary to implement their perspectives outside their particular group"* (Collins, 2000, p. 185). So gaining access to the equitable potentials of the Internet to empower women and resist dominant structures may be temporary gains in that the resources needed to sustain this empowerment may not exist, and the Million Woman March is an example of this temporary empowerment.

6.2 EFFECTING CHANGE IN XBOX LIVE

It is possible for dominant audiences who consume video game content to resist the stereotypical representations within the narrative. While recognizing some of the correlations between the encoding and decoding of representation, Hall (1996) constructs three hypothetical positions: dominant-hegemonic, negotiated, and oppositional. Tania Modleski (1986) nicely summarizes these three positions: the dominant response to the reading of text accepts its message at face value; the negotiated response may dispute a particular claim but accepts its overall interpretation; and the oppositional response rejects the dominant interpretations in the interest of the oppressed. In short, while reading representations, people do not necessarily accept the dominant interpretations (the dominant-hegemonic responses) that benefit the dominant but can negotiate with them (negotiated responses) or reject them (oppositional responses). Even though the system of representation enables the dominant to classify, control, and naturalize certain knowledge as the truth, people do not necessarily accept such knowledge, nor do they necessarily become bearers of power/knowledge, though they can become agents of resistance. So black women, by resisting the dominant's interpretations and rejecting them completely, recognize that they have the ability and control to challenge the previous narrative deployed of them. This reflects the first tenet of black feminist thought of self-definition.

Women are no longer objecting themselves to the representations so often disseminated through the media: the stereotypical images of mammies, matriarchs, welfare recipients, and hot mommas (Collins, 2000, p. 69). This has a pervading focal point in black feminist thought and these images are controlled by the dominant so resisting this is imperative. The purpose of these images, as Collins (2000, p. 69) explains, is to make intersecting inequalities appear to be natural, normal, and inevitable parts of everyday life.

The second tenet of Hill Collins' theory is the intersecting reality of black women. As she argues, being black and female in the United States continues to expose African-American women to certain common experiences (Collins, 2000, p. 23). So continuing the struggle of confronting and dismantling structures of domination in terms of race, class, and gender is still imperative (Taylor, 1998, p. 235). Women in Xbox Live continually express the conflation of their identities into one body with on intersecting reality. Her identities cannot be separated. They are all important. And they all work to create a hostile reality for her within Xbox Live, as in physical spaces both public and private.

Third, black women simultaneously address intellectual thought in the spirit of political activism. As this text illustrated, black women work diligently to address the oppressions they experience and identify meaningful solutions to empower themselves within the space. Although these solutions and strategies have yet to effect significant change within Xbox Live, they are empowered knowing that they have done something.

The last theme of black feminist thought is that "Black women recognize a distinct cultural heritage that gives them the energy and skills to resist and transform daily discrimination" (Taylor, 1998, p. 235). Historically, W.E.B. DuBois and Frantz Fanon both wrote on the reception of blackness. DuBois speaks of the "double consciousness" of blackness and the veil that African Americans must look through, seeing themselves "through the eyes of others." This "second sight" of which DuBois writes is a double-edged sword, at once a gift in duality, but also a severe hindrance toward the making of the self, and DuBois's pronouncement of the marking of the twentieth century by the "color line" still defines race relations in America. Incorporating additional lenses of oppression (gender, class, sexuality, religion, citizenship status, etc.) adds to the frames in which marginalized bodies must peer each day.

These themes remind black women of the necessity to understand the power relations that dominate and pervade their daily lives. According to Hardiman and Jackson (1997, p. 17) the following four key elements are in place in social oppression:

1. The power to define and name reality resides in the dominant group. Also it is the dominant group who determines what is "normal," "real," or correct.
2. Acts of harassment, discrimination, exploitation, marginalization, and any other form of differential and unequal treatment are systematic and embedded in the institutions.
3. Oppression is internalized by the individual.
4. The dominant culture is imposed and the target group's culture, language, and history are misrepresented, distorted, or discounted.

These factors are both present and perpetuate the condition of oppression of marginalized groups in society. Audre Lorde's use of the word "dismantle" is significant to the ability for marginalized groups to sustain their empowerment. Lorde did not use "destroy," which would imply an annihilation of hegemonic control. "Dismantle" suggests the breaking down into parts, not the total destruction of those elements. Dismantling could also mean that, at some other time, those singular entities could very well form again into a cohesive whole, although not necessarily modeling the previous form. I interrogate these various word choices because they offer a lens through which to analyze the tools used by the women within the text.

By the frameworks and concepts created through social movement theory, resource mobilization theory, and literature on digital activism, the efforts employed by women of color within Xbox Live are futile, short lived, and have limited ability to effect significant change. However, who decides if a strategy or tactic is successful or not? Any work that interrogates the reality of marginalized populations is significant. Anything reality that privileges the lived experiences of the oppressed is needed. bell hooks contends, "As subjects, people have the right to define their own reality, establish their own identities, name their history. As objects, one's reality is defined by others, one's identity is created by others, one's history named only in ways that define one's relationship to those who are subject" (as cited in Collins, 2000, p. 69). The conception of this text is a testament to their struggles within Xbox Live. We need more researchers to privilege the experiences of women, people of color, sexual minorities, immigrants, and other marginalized populations to situate their realities within the larger context of inequality, injustice, and oppression.

As alluded to in this chapter, "using the master's tools" provides a way to re-center racism, sexism, and other inequalities, but this does not mean that the tools can tear these "isms" apart. Under racism, sexism, class exploitation, heterosexism, and similar systems of oppression, elite groups use their power to uphold privilege through the economic political or ideological domination of blacks, women, poor people, and LGBT people. This perspective sees power relations as a zero-sum game—one in which less powerful people gain power when it is redistributed to them from more powerful groups (Collins, 2006, p. 21). Waiting for the powerful to allocate equal access to subordinate groups often leads to resistance, which can mean taking the power often by force, revolt, or revolution (Collins, 2006). As black women, we have to understand the historical basis of our lived experiences and identify meaningful solutions to combat and resist continued discrimination, oppression, and inequality. One of the first steps necessary in identifying these solutions is to devote more scholarship and research on black women as objects of study—make black women visible.

BIBLIOGRAPHY

Adichie, C. (2009). The danger of a single story. *TED Ideas Worth Spreading*.

Ahuja, M. K., & Carley, K. M. (1998). Network structure in virtual organizations. *Journal of Computer-Mediated Communication, 3*. Available from <http://dx.doi.org/10.1111/j.1083-6101>.

Anzaldúa, G. E. (1987). *Borderlands/La Frontera: The new mestiza*. San Francisco, CA: Aunt Lute Books.

Aveni, A. F. (1978). Organizational linkages and resource mobilization: The significance of linkage strength and breadth. *The Sociological Quarterly, 19*(2), 185–202.

Barrett, P. (2006). White thumbs, black bodies: Race, violence, and neoliberal fantasies in grand theft auto: San Andreas. *The Review of Education Pedagogy and Cultural Studies, 28*(1), 95–119.

Bartle, R. (1996). Hearts, clubs, diamonds, spades: Players who suit MUDs. *Journal of MUD Research, 1*(1), 19.

Baugh, J. (2003). Linguistic profiling. In S. Makoni, G. Smitherman, & A. S. Ball (Eds.), *Black linguistics: Language, society, and politics in Africa and the Americas* (pp. 155–168). New York, NY: Routledge.

Beasley, B., & Standley, T. C. (2002). Shirts vs. skins: Clothing as an indicator of gender role stereotyping in video games. *Mass Communication & Society, 5*, 279–293.

Berlin, I. (1998). *Many thousands gone: The first two centuries of slavery in North America*. Harvard University Press.

Bogost, I. (2006). Videogames and ideological frames. *Popular Communication, 4*(3), 165–183.

Bonchek, M. S. (1995, April). Grassroots in cyberspace: Using computer networks to facilitate political participation. In *53rd annual meeting of the Midwest Political Science Association* (Vol. 6), Chicago, IL.

Bourdieu, P. (1984). *Distinction: A social critique of the judgment of taste* (R. Nice, Trans.) Cambridge, MA: Harvard University Press.

Brainard, L. A., & Siplon, P. D. (2000, August). Cyberspace challenges to mainstream advocacy groups: The case of health care activism. In *Annual meeting of the American Political Science Association*, Marriot Wardman Park.

Brock, A. (2011). "When keeping it real goes wrong": Resident Evil 5, racial representation, and gamers. *Games and Culture, 6*(5), 429–452.

Brookey, R. A. (2009). Paradise crashed: Rethinking MMORPG's and other virtual worlds. An introduction. *Critical Studies in Media Communication, 2*(26), 101–103.

Bucholz, M. (1999). You da man: Narrating the racial other in the production of white masculinity. *Journal of Sociolinguistics, 3*(4), 443–460.

Calhoun, C. (1993). "New social movements" of the early nineteenth century. *Social Science History, 17*(3), 385–427.

Castañeda Peña, H., Salazar Sierra, A., González Romero, N., Sierra Gutiérrez, L. I., & Menéndez Echavarría, A. (2013). Profiling academic research on massively multiplayer on-line role-play gaming (MMORPG) 2000-2009: Horizons for educational research. *Folios, 38*, 75–94.

Chan, D. (2005). Playing with race: The ethics of racialized representations in e-games. *International Review of Information Ethics, 4*(12), 24–30.

Clinard, M. B., & Meier, R. F. (1998). *Sociology of deviant behavior* (10th ed.). Fort Worth, TX: Harcourt Brace.

Coakley, J. (1994). *Sport in society: Issues and controversies.* New York, NY: McGraw-Hill.

Cohen, J. L. (1985). Strategy or identity: New theoretical paradigms and contemporary social movements. *Social Research, 52*(4), 663–716.

Collins, P. H. (1998). It's all in the family: Intersections of gender, race, and nation. *Hypatia, 13* (3), 62–82.

Collins, P. H. (2000). The social construction of black feminist thought. In J. James & T. D. Sharpley-Whiting (Eds.), *The black feminist reader* (pp. 183–207). Oxford: Wiley-Blackwell.

Collins, P. H. (2006). *From Black power to hip hop: Racism, nationalism, and feminism.* Philadelphia, PA: Temple University Press.

Connell, R. W. (1995). *Masculinities.* Berkeley, CA: University of California Press.

Connell, R. (2001). The social organization of masculinity. In S. Whitehead & F. Barrett (Eds.), *The masculinities reader* (pp. 30–48). Cambridge, MA: Polity Press.

Connell, R. W., & Messerschmidt, J. W. (2005). Hegemonic masculinity: Rethinking the concept. *Gender & Society, 19*(6), 829–859.

Crecente, B. (2011). *Dead Island maker gives leading lady a "feminist whore" skill.* Kotaku. <http://kotaku.com/5838387/dead-island-maker-gives-leading-lady-a-feminist-whore-skill> Accessed 03.01.14.

Crenshaw, K. (1989). Demarginalizing the intersection of race and sex: A Black feminist critique of antidiscrimination doctrine, feminist theory and antiracist politics. *The University of Chicago Legal Forum, 140*, 139–167.

Crenshaw, K. (1991). Mapping the margins: Intersectionality, identity politics, and violence against women of color. *Stanford Law Review, 43*(6), 1241–1299.

Crow, B., & Longford, M. (2004). Digital activism in Canada. In *Seeking convergence in policy and practice: Communications in the public interest* (Vol. 2, pp. 349–362).

Davis, A. (1983). *Women, race, and class.* New York, NY: Vintage.

Deaux, K., & Stewart, A. (2001). Framing gendered identities. In R. Unger (Ed.), *Handbook of the psychology of women and gender.* New York, NY: John Wiley & Sons.

Denzin, N. K. (1995). *The cinematic society: The voyeur's gaze* (Vol. 34). Thousand Oaks: Sage.

Description of Xbox 360 gamer profiles. Xbox. Retrieved from: <http://support.xbox.com/support/en/us/nxe/kb.aspx?ID=905882&lcid=1033&category=xboxlive> Accessed 22.11.09.

Dill, K., & Thill, K. (2007). Video game characters and the socialization of gender roles: Young people's perception mirror sexist media depictions. *Sex Roles, 57*, 851–864.

Downs, E., & Smith, S. L. (2009). Keeping abreast of hypersexuality: A video game character content analysis. *Sex Roles, 62*, 721–733.

Dukes, R., & Martinez, R. (1994). The impact of ethgender on self-esteem among adolescents. *Adolescence, 29*, 105–116.

Eltantawy, N., & Wiest, J. B. (2011). Social media in the Egyptian revolution: Reconsidering resource mobilization theory. *International Journal of Communication, 5*, 1207–1224.

ESA (2008). *Essential facts about games and violence.* Entertainment Software Association.

ESA (2012). *Essential facts about the computer and video game industry.* Entertainment Software Association.

Everett, A. (2009). *Digital diaspora.* Albany, NY: SUNY Press.

Ewick, P., & Silbey, S. (1995). Subversive stories and hegemonic tales: Toward a sociology of narrative. *Law & Society Review, 29*(2), 197–226.

Ferdman, B., & Gallegos, P. (2001). Racial identity development and Latino/as in the United States. In C. Wijeyesinghe & B. Jackson (Eds.), *New perspectives on racial identity development* (pp. 32–66). New York, NY: New York University Press.

Ferrell, J., & Websdale, N. (1996). Materials for making trouble. In J. Ferrell & N. Websdale (Eds.), *Making trouble: Cultural constructions of crime, deviance, and control* (pp. 3–21). New Brunswick, NJ: Transaction Publishers.

Flanagan, M. (2005) Troubling 'games for girls': Notes from the edge of game design. In *DiGRA 2005 conference: Changing views—worlds in play.* Available from < http://www.digra.org/dl/db/ 06278.14520.pdf >.

Foo, C. Y., & Koivisto, E. M. (2004). Defining grief play in MMORPGs: Player and developer perceptions. In *The Australasian computing education conference* (Vol. 74, pp. 245–250), Singapore.

Foster, I., Kesselman, C., & Tuecke, S. (2001). The anatomy of the grid: Enabling scalable virtual organizations. *International Journal of High Performance Computing Applications, 15*(3), 200–222.

Frankenberg, R. (1993). *White women, race matters: The social construction of whiteness.* Minneapolis, MN: University of Minnesota Press.

Frasier, A. (2009, January 20). *Black people don't play video games.* The Koalition. Retrieved from < http://www.thekoalition.com/black-people-dont-play-video-games > Accessed 22.11.09.

Friesen, B. (2004). Book review: Contested knowledge: Social theory today. *Teaching Sociology, 32*(3), 333–335.

Fron, J., Fullerton, T., Morie, J. F., & Pearce, C. (2007, September). The hegemony of play. In: *Situated play: Proceedings of Digital Games Research Association 2007 conference* (pp. 1–10), Tokyo, Japan.

Gamson, W. A. (1975). *The strategy of social protest* (pp. 89–109). Homewood, IL: Dorsey Press.

Garrett, R. K. (2006). Protest in an information society: A review of literature on social movements and new ICTs. *Information Communication & Society, 9*(2), 202–224.

Geddes, R. (2008, October 9). *IGN: TGS 2008: Avatars required.* IGN. Retrieved from < http:// xboxlive.ign.com/articles/918/918113p1.html > Accessed 22.11.09.

Germond-Duret, C. (2012). From avatar to reality: Development, environment and the representation of Cameroonian Pygmies. *International Journal on Minority and Group Rights, 19*(2), 129–151.

Gibson, J. W. (1996). The social construction of whiteness in Shellcracker Haven, Florida. *Human Organization, 55*(4), 379–389.

Goffman, E. (1963). *Stigma: Notes on the management of spoiled identity.* Englewood Cliffs, NJ: Prentice Hall.

Good, O. (2011, April 2). *Nielsen survey finds black gamers spend the most time playing consoles.* Kotaku. Retrieved from < http://kotaku.com/5788268/nielsen-survey-finds-black-gamers-spend-the-most-time-playing-consoles > Accessed 18.12.13.

Gramsci, A. (1971). *Selections from the prison notebooks of Antonio Gramsci.* New York, NY: International Publishers.

Gray, K. (2011). *Deviant bodies resisting online: Examining the intersecting realities of women of color in Xbox Live*. Doctoral dissertation, Arizona State University.

Gray, K. L. (2012). Diffusion of innovation theory and Xbox Live examining minority gamers' responses and rate of adoption to changes in Xbox Live. *Bulletin of Science Technology & Society, 32*(6), 463–470.

Gray, K. L., & Buente, W. (2014). 'What's in a name?' Applying social information processing theory to gamertag identification in Xbox Live, Manuscript in Preparation.

Grenier, R., & Metes, G. (1995). *Going virtual: Moving your organization into the 21st century.* Upper Saddle River, NJ: Prentice Hall PTR.

Hafner, K. (2004, October 14). What do women game designers want? *The New York Times.*

Hall, S. (1980). Cultural studies: Two paradigms. *Media Culture & Society, 2*(1), 57–72.

Hall, S. (1996). Gramsci's relevance for the study of race and ethnicity. In *Stuart Hall: Critical Dialogues in Cultural Studies* (pp. 411–440).

Hall, S. (Ed.), (1997). *Representation: Cultural representations and signifying practices* (Vol. 2). Thousand Oaks: Sage.

Hardiman, R., & Jackson, B. W. (1997). Conceptual foundations for social justice courses. *Teaching for diversity and social justice: A sourcebook* (pp. 16–29).

Harnois, C. (2010). Race, gender, and the black women's standpoint. *Sociological Forum, 25*(1), 68–85.

Haythornthwaite, C., & Wellman, B. (2004). The Internet in everyday life. *Journal of Communication, 54*(3), 571–574.

Hebdige, D. (1979). *Subculture: The meaning of style.* London: Methuen.

Holt, L. (2008). Embodied social capital and geographic perspectives: Performing the habitus. *Progress in Human Geography, 32*(2), 227.

Jansz, J., & Martis, R. G. (2007). The Lara phenomenon: Powerful female characters in video games. *Sex Roles, 56*(3), 141–148.

Jefferies, V., & Ransford, H. (1980). *Social stratification: A multiple hierarchy approach.* Boston, MA: Allyn & Bacon.

Jenkins, J. C. (1983). Resource mobilization theory and the study of social movements. *Annual Review of Sociology, 9*, 527–553.

Jenkins, H. (2006). *Convergence culture: Where old and new media collide.* New York, NY: New York University Press.

Joinson, A. (2001). Self-disclosure in computer mediated communication: The role of self-awareness and visual anonymity. *European Journal of Social Psychology, 31*, 177–192.

Joseph, R. L. (2009). "Tyra banks is fat": Reading (post-) racism and (post-) feminism in the new millennium. *Critical Studies in Media Communication, 3*(26), 237–254.

Juul, J. (2002). Time to play—an examination of game temporality. In *First person: New media as story, performance, and game*. Massachusetts: MIT Press.

Kennedy, H. (2002). Lara Croft, feminist icon or cyber bimbo: The limits of textual analysis. *Game Studies, 2*(2). Available from <http://www.gamestudies.org/0202/kennedy/>.

Kimmel, M. (1996). *Manhood in America: A cultural history.* New York, NY: The Free Press.

Kolko, B. (2000). Erasing @race: Going white in the (inter)face. In B. Kolko, L. Nakamura, & G. B. Rodman (Eds.), *Race in cyberspace.* New York, NY: Routledge.

Kristof, A. L., Brown, K. G., Sims, H. P., Jr., & Smith, K. A. (1995). The virtual team: A case study and inductive model. In M. M. Beyerlein, D. A. Johnson, & S. T. Beyerlein (Eds.),

Advances in interdisciplinary studies of work teams: Knowledge work in teams (Vol. 2, pp. 229–253). Greenwich, CT: JAI Press.

Langman, L. (2005). From virtual public spheres to global justice: A critical theory of Internetworked social movements. *Sociological Theory, 23*(1), 42–74.

Laraña, E., Johnston, H., & Gusfield, J. R. (Eds.), (1994). *New social movements: From ideology to identity.* Philadelphia, PA: Temple University Press.

Leizerov, S. (2000). Privacy advocacy groups versus Intel: A case study of how social movements are tactically using the Internet to fight corporations. *Social Science Computer Review, 18*(4), 461–483.

Leonard, D. (2003). "Live in your world, play in ours": Race, video games, and consuming the other. *Studies in Media & Information Literacy Education, 3*(4), 1–9.

Leonard, D. J. (2004). High tech blackface—race, sports video games and becoming the other. *Intelligent Agent, 4*(4.2), 1–5.

Leonard, D. J. (2006). Not a hater, just keepin' it real: The importance of race and gender based game studies. *Games and Culture, 1*(1), 83–88.

Levy, D. (2007). Hegemonic masculinity. In M. Flood, J. K. Gardiner, B. Pease, & K. Pringle (Eds.), *Encyclopedia of men and masculinities* (pp. 253–254). London: Routledge.

Lin, H., & Sun, C. T. (2005). White-eyed and griefer player culture: Deviance construction in MMORPGs. *Worlds in Play: International Perspectives on Digital Games Research, 21,* 103.

Lipnack, J., & Stamps, J. (1997). *Virtual teams: Reaching across space, time and organizations with technology.* New York, NY: John Wiley.

Lorde, A. (1981/2009). The uses of anger: Women responding to racism. In S. M. James, F. S. Foster, & B. Guy-Sheftall (Eds.), *Still brave: The evolution of black women's studies* (pp. 23–29). New York, NY: The Feminist Press.

Maanen, J. V. (1988). *Tales of the field: On writing ethnography.* Chicago, IL: University of Chicago Press.

Marcia, J. E. (1966). Development and validation of ego identity status. *Journal of Personality and Social Psychology, 5,* 551–558.

Marriott, M. (2004, August 23). *Popular video games play on racial stereotypes, critics say.* The San Diego Union-Tribune. Retrieved from <http://www.signonsandiego.com/uniontrib/20040823/news_mz1b23video> Accessed 05.12.10.

Martinez, R., & Dukes, R. (1991). Ethnic and gender differences in self-esteem. *Youth and Society, 22,* 318–338.

McAdam, D. (1988). *Freedom summer.* New York, NY: Oxford University Press.

McCarthy, J. D., & Zald, M. N. (1977). Resource mobilization and social movements: A partial theory. *American Journal of Sociology, 82,* 1212–1241.

McLaughlin, R. (2008, February 29). *IGN presents: The history of Tomb Raider.* IGN. Retrieved from <http://www.ign.com/articles/2008/03/01/ign-presents-the-history-of-tomb-raider> Accessed 22.01.14.

McQuivey, J. (2001). The digital locker room: The young, white male as center of the video gaming universe. In E. Toth & L. Aldoory (Eds.), *The gender challenge to media: Diverse voices from the field* (pp. 183–214). Cresskill, NJ: Hampton Press, Inc.

Melucci, A. (1989). *Nomads of the present: Social movements and individual needs in contemporary society.* Philadelphia, PA: Temple University Press.

Meyer, D. S., & Tarrow, S. G. (Eds.), (1998). *The social movement society: Contentious politics for a new century.* Lanham, MD: Rowman & Littlefield.

Miller, M. K., & Summers, A. (2007). Gender differences in video game characters' roles, appearances, and attire as portrayed in video game magazines. *Sex Roles, 57,* 733−742.

Modleski, T. (Ed.), (1986). *Studies in entertainment: critical approaches to mass culture* (Vol. 7). Indiana University Press.

Mohanram, R. (1999). *Black body: Women, colonialism, and space.* Minneapolis, MN: University of Minnesota Press.

Mowshowitz, A. (1997). On the theory of virtual organization. *Systems Research and Behavioral Science, 14*(6), 373−384.

Mulvey, L. (1975). Visual pleasure and narrative cinema. *Screen, 16,* 6−18.

Myers, D. J. (2000). The diffusion of collective violence: Infectiousness, susceptibility, and mass media networks. *American Journal of Sociology, 106*(1), 173−208.

Myers, D. (2007, September). Self and selfishness in online social play. In *Situated play, proceedings of DiGRA 2007 conference* (pp. 226−234), Tokyo.

Myers, M. (2010). *Gears of War 3: Adding a female character?* The Boston Phoenix. Retrieved from <http://thephoenix.com/blogs/laserorgy/archive/2010/03/31/gears-of-war-3-adding-a-female-character.aspx> Accessed 10.11.10.

Nakamura, L. (2002). *Cybertypes: Race, ethnicity and identity on the Internet.* London: Routledge.

Nakamura, L. (2009). Don't hate the player, hate the game: The racialization of labor in world of warcraft. *Critical Studies in Media Communication, 26*(2), 128−144.

Newman, D. (2008). *Sociology: Exploring the architecture of everyday life* (7th ed.). Thousand Oaks, CA: Pine Forge Press.

Oberschall, A. (1973). *Social conflict and social movements.* Englewood Cliffs, NJ: Prentice Hall.

Omi, M., & Winant, H. (1994). *Racial formation in the United States: From the 1960s to the 1990s.* New York, NY: Routledge.

Pesquera, B. M., & Segura, D. A. (1997). There is no going back: Chicanas and feminism. *Chicana feminist thought: The basic historical writings* (pp. 294−309).

Pinchefsky, C. (2013). *A feminist reviews Tomb Raider's Lara Croft.* Forbes. <http://www.forbes.com/sites/carolpinchefsky/2013/03/12/a-feminist-reviews-tomb-raiders-lara-croft/print/> Accessed 22.12.13.

Poor, N. (2005). Mechanisms of an online public sphere: The website Slashdot. *Journal of Computer Mediated Communication, 10*(2), article 4. Retrieved from <http://jcmc.indiana.edu/vol10/issue2/poor.html> Accessed 3.12.13.

Quinn, S. (2005). Convergence's fundamental question. *Journalism Studies, 6,* 29−38.

Razack, S. (2002). Gendered racial violence and spatialized justice: The murder of Pamela George. In S. Razack (Ed.), *Race space and the law: Unmapping a white settler society* (pp. 121−156). Toronto: Between the Lines.

Razack, S., & Fellow, M. (1998). Race to innocence: Confronting hierarchical relationships among women. *Gender Race & Justice, 1*(2), 335−352.

Reay, D. (2004). "It's all becoming a habitus": Beyond the habitual use of habitus in educational research. *British Journal of Sociology of Education, 25*(4), 431−444.

Roebuck, J. B., & Neff, R. L. (1980). The multiple reality of the "redneck": Toward a grounded theory of the southern class structure. *Studies in Symbolic Interaction, 3,* 233−262.

Roediger, D. R. (1991). *The wages of whiteness: Race and the making of the American working class.* London: Verso.

Rogers, E. M., & Singhal, A. (2003). Empowerment and communication: Lessons learned from organizing for social change. *Communication Yearbook, 27*, 67–86.

Said, E. (1978). *Orientalism*. New York, NY: Pantheon.

Smith, J. H. (2004). Playing dirty—Understanding conflicts in multiplayer games. In *Paper presented at the 5th annual conference of the Association of Internet Researchers* (pp. 1–15). Sussex: The University of Sussex.

Stewart, A. J., & McDermott, C. (2004). Gender in psychology. *Annual Review of Psychology, 55*, 519–544.

Suler, J. (2004). The online disinhibition effect. *Cyber Psychology and Behavior, 7*(3), 321–326.

Suler, J., & Phillips, W. (1998). The bad boys of cyberspace: Deviant behavior in multimedia chat communities. *CyberPsychology and Behavior, 1*, 275–294.

Tajfel, H., & Turner, J. C. (1985). The social identity theory of intergroup behavior. In S. Worchel & W. G. Austin (Eds.), *Psychology of intergroup relations* (2nd ed., pp. 7–24). Chicago, IL: Nelson-Hall.

Tarrow, S. (1998). *Power in movement: Social movements, collective action, and politics* (2nd ed.). New York, NY: Cambridge University Press.

Taylor, U. (1998). The historical evolution of black feminist theory and praxis. *Journal of Black Studies, 29*(2), 234–253.

Taylor, V., & Whittier, N. E. (1992). Collective identity in social movement communities: Lesbian feminist mobilization. In *Social perspectives in lesbian and gay studies* (1998, pp. 349–365). New York, NY: Routledge.

Terry, J., & Urla, J. (1995). *Deviant bodies: Critical perspectives on difference in science and popular culture*. Bloomington, IN: Indiana University Press.

Thompsen, P. (2003). What's fueling the flames in cyberspace? A social influence model. In L. Strate, R. L. Jacobson, & S. Gibson (Eds.), *Communication and cyberspace: Social interaction in an electronic environment* (2nd ed., pp. 329–347). Cresskill, NJ: Hampton Press, Inc.

Thorsen, T. (2009, January 6). *28 million Xbox 360s sold, 17 million on Xbox Live*. Gamespot. Retrieved from < http://www.gamespot.com/news/6202733.html > Accessed 11.09.

Travica, B. (2005). Information view of organization. *Journal of International Technology and Information Management, 14*(3), 1–20.

Uhler Cart, C. (1997). Online computer networks: Potential and challenges for community organizing and community building now and in the future. In M. Minkler (Ed.), *Community organizing and community building for health* (pp. 325–338). New Brunswick, NJ: Rutgers University Press.

Vegh, S. (2003). Classifying forms of online activism: The case of cyberprotests against the World Bank. In M. McCaughey & M. Ayers (Eds.), *Cyberactivism online activism in theory and practice* (pp. 71–96). London: Routledge.

Vera, H., & De los Santos, E. (2005). Chicana identity construction: Pushing the boundaries. *Journal of Hispanic Higher Education, 4*(2), 102–113.

Vera, H., & Gordon, A. M. (2003). The beautiful American: Sincere fictions of the White messiah in Hollywood movies. In A. W. Doanne & E. Bonilla-Silva (Eds.), *White out: The continuing significance of racism* (pp. 113–125). New York, NY: Routledge.

Wacquant, L. (1998). Pierre Bourdieu. In R. Stones (Ed.), *Key sociological thinkers* (pp. 215–229). London: Macmillan Press.

Wadley, G., Gibbs, M., Hew, K., & Graham, C. (2003, November). Computer supported cooperative play, "Third places" and online videogames. In S. Viller & P. Wyeth (Eds.), *Proceedings of the thirteenth Australian conference on computer human interaction* (pp. 238–241). Brisbane, Australia: University of Queensland.

Ware, N. (2010). You must defeat Shen Long to stand a chance: Street fighter, race, play, and player. Master's thesis, Bowling Green State University. Retrieved from < http://etd.ohiolink. edu/send-pdf.cgi/Ware%20Nicholas%20R.pdf?bgsu1277062605 > Accessed 18.11.13.

Warner, D., & Raiter, M. (2005). Social context in massively-multiplayer online games (MMOGs): Ethical questions in shared space. *International Review of Information Ethics*, *4*(7), 46–52.

Webb, S. (2001). Avatar culture: Narrative, power, and identity in virtual world environments. *Information, Communication, & Society*, *4*(4), 560–594.

Wellman, B. (2002). *Living networked in the wired world*. Brisbane, Australia: International Sociological Association (ISA).

Wellman, B., Hasse, A. Q., Witte, J., & Hampton, K. (2001). Does the Internet increase, decrease, or supplement social capital? Social networks, participation, and community commitment. *American Behavioral Scientist*, *45*(3), 436–455.

Whitten, M. (2010, February 5). *An open letter from Xbox Live General Manager Marc Whitten*. Microsoft. Retrieved from < http://www.xbox.com/en-US/press/2010/0205-whittenletter.htm > Accessed 5.12.10.

Wright, J. K. (2010). *Stagolees, superflies, & gangsta rappers: Black masculinity, bad men, and the struggle for power*. Doctoral dissertation, Howard University.

Wyatt, V. (1993). *The science book for girls and other intelligent beings*. Toronto: Kids Can Press.

Yee, N. (2004). *Avatar and identity. The Daedalus Gateway: The Psychology of MMORPGs*. Retrieved from < http://www.nickyee.com/daedalus/gateway_identity.html > Accessed 5.12.10.

Yegenoglu, M. (1998). *Colonial fantasies: Towards a feminist reading of orientalism*. Cambridge University Press.

Yu, S. L. (2004). Orientalist fantasy and desire in Maxine Hong Kingston's the Woman Warrior. In E. Marino & B. Simal (Eds.), *National, communal and personal voices in Asian America and the Asian diaspora* (pp. 67–86). Berlin: Lit Verlag.

BIBLIOGRAPHY

Black Ops Entertainment (2002). Street Hoops *[Xbox]*. Santa Monica, CA: Activision.

Blizzard Entertainment (2004). World of Warcraft *[PC]*. Irvine, CA: Blizzard Entertainment.

Bungie Studios (2004). Halo 2 *[Xbox]*. Redmond, WA: Microsoft Game Studios.

Capcom (2009). Resident Evil 5 *[Xbox 360]*. Osaka, Japan: Capcom.

Crystal Dynamics (2013). Tomb Raider *[Xbox 360]*. Tokyo, Japan: Square Enix.

Dimps & Capcom (2009). Street Fighter IV *[Xbox 360]*. Osaka, Japan: Capcom.

DMA Designs (2001). Grand Theft Auto III *[Xbox]*. New York, NY: Rockstar Games.

EA Canada (2005). NBA Street V3 *[Xbox]*. Redwood City, CA: EA Big.

EA Tiburon (2004). NFL Street *[Xbox]*. Redwood City, CA: Electronic Arts.

Epic Games (2006). Gears of War *[Xbox 360]*. Redmond, WA: Microsoft Studios.

Epic Games (2008). Gears of War 2 *[Xbox 360]*. Redmond, WA: Microsoft Studios.

Epic Games (2011). Gears of War 3 *[Xbox 360]*. Redmond, WA: Microsoft Studios.

Exald Entertainment (2005). True Crime: New York City *[Xbox]*. Santa Monica, CA: Activision.

iD Software (1993). Doom *[PC]*. New York, NY: GT Interactive Software.

iD Software (1996). Quake *[PC]*. New York, NY: GT Interactive Software.

Infinity Ward (2007). Call of Duty 4: Modern Warfare *[Xbox 360]*. Santa Monica, CA: Activision.

Luxoflux (2004). True Crime: Streets of L.A. *[Xbox]*. Santa Monica, CA: Activision.

Rockstar North (2002). Grand Theft Auto: Vice CIty *[Xbox]*. New York, NY: Rockstar Games.

Rockstar North (2004). Grand Theft Auto: San Andreas *[Xbox]*. New York, NY: Rockstar Games.

Rockstar North (2013). Grand Theft Auto V *[Xbox 360]*. New York, NY: Rockstar Games.

Sony Online Entertainment (1999). EverQuest *[PC]*. San Diego, CA: Sony Online Entertainment.

Techland (2011). Dead Island *[Xbox 360]*. Planegg, Germany: Deep Silver.

Techland (2013). Dead Island: Riptide *[Xbox 360]*. Planegg, Germany: Deep Silver.

CPSIA information can be obtained
at www.ICGtesting.com
Printed in the USA
FSOW03n1827140816
23698FS